4-Star Retirement

2-Star Budget

By

Jim Olson

4-Star Retirement – 2-Star Budget

Copyright 2013 by Jim Olson

All rights reserved. No part of this book may be used or reproduced in any manner whatsoever without written permission from Jim Olson, except as provided by the United States of America copyright law or in the case of brief quotations embodied in articles and reviews.

The scanning, uploading and distribution of this book via the Internet or via any other means without the permission of the publisher is illegal and punishable by law.

Please purchase only authorized electronic editions and do not participate in or encourage electronic piracy of copyrighted materials. Your support of the author's rights is sincerely appreciated.

Printed in the United States of America.

ISBN: 978-1-935723-86-8

Dedication

To my wonderful wife, Jean.

Her financial magic

has made our 58 years of marriage

and 15 years of retirement

a huge success.

Acknowledgements

Ann McIndoo, my Author's Coach, who you can find at <u>www.SoYouWantToWrite.com</u>. Ann has been a jewel in helping this book become a reality. Her guidance for content, layout and cover were indispensable.

To Joe & Betty,

A great couple who portray the best of retirements.

Jim Olson

Contents

	Page
Introduction	ix
Chapter One: Deciding to Retire	1
Chapter Two: Where to Retire?	5
Chapter Three: A Hut or a Mansion?	11
Chapter Four: Are Your Finances Ready?	21
Chapter Five: Managing Finances in Retirement	31
Chapter Six: You Control the Budget	37
Chapter Seven: Income-Timing-Lifestyle	41
a) Forced Retirement	42
b) Voluntary Early Retirement	47
c) Normal Retirement Age	54
Chapter Eight: Taxes Matter in Retirement	57
Chapter Nine: Making Every Dollar Count	67
Chapter Ten: Healthy Retirement	73
Chapter Eleven: Affordable Fun in Retirement	89

Chapter Twelve: Travel in Retirement 97

Chapter Thirteen: Plan Your Estate 109

Chapter Fourteen: Benefits of Giving Back 117

Chapter Fifteen: Workable Retirement Philosophies 121

Resources 123

Introduction

What do you need to achieve for a successful retirement? Whether you are 40 or 65, you need solid retirement decisions. With the guidance provided by 4 STAR RETIREMENT-2 STAR BUDGET, you can achieve your desired retirement lifestyle. The book is designed with stand-alone chapters, allowing the reader to focus on the most applicable retirement topics.

Chapter One covers your retirement decision.

Chapter Two will help you decide where is the best place to live, from staying where you are to moving overseas.

Chapter Three explores the pros and cons of various types of dwellings available to you. Should you live in your current home, hit the road in an RV or move to your recreation property at the lake?

Chapter Four introduces alternative investments and savings programs, so you will be able to retire when you wish.

Chapter Five will assist your handling and investing of funds in retirement, so your assets will last as long as you do.

Chapter Six provides budgeting and cost control techniques, helping you live a good life in retirement without a huge bucket of money.

Chapter Seven will give you ideas on how to supplement your retirement income.

Chapter Eight offers suggestions for methods you can utilize to increase your cash flow through efficient use of legal income tax options.

Chapter Nine explores how to be a good shepherd of your funds, making every dollar count.

Chapter Ten will provide ways to maintain your health in retirement.

Chapter Eleven is devoted to ways you can have affordable fun in retirement.

Chapter Twelve handles traveling in retirement, with ways to afford your travel dreams.

Chapter Thirteen explores the many important steps necessary for your estate planning.

Chapter Fourteen provides ways you can give back to your community, not only with money, but through managerial and professional skills.

Chapter Fifteen presents a few meaningful philosophies designed to keep your retirement years the best and most enjoyable ever.

Jim Olson

2013

Chapter One

Deciding to Retire

Retirement is a very personal thing, and it should be tailored to your lifestyle and what it means to you. Although a long and enjoyable retirement may be high on the list of your goals, less than one person in five has a written statement of what they want in retirement and how to successfully achieve it.

To get you into the right frame of mind, let's do a little exercise I call, "My Retirement Expectations." You and your partner each make a separate short statement about what you want in retirement in these categories:

☆ Recreation
☆ Travel
☆ Education
☆ Volunteering
☆ Income Supplements
☆ Health & Fitness
☆ Hobbies
☆ Financial Management
☆ Time Together

Know what you want and what you expect from retirement. If you are in the typical retirement age of 60 to 65, your retirement will likely last 25 to 30 years, so maintain flexibility in your expectations. Your interests and capabilities change as you age, so it is important before you retire to picture your initial retirement lifestyle. Reconcile any differences in your list of expectations between you and your partner, then take charge of your retirement. Have a definite game plan, because without a plan you will be like "Alice In Wonderland," who was told, "If you don't care where you are going, I guess anywhere will do."

Your expectations may include golf twice or three times per week, gardening, reading, fishing. Your travel plans involve seeing North America, cruising the world or spending time in South or Central America. You may decide to complete your college degree, which was dropped when you married. You may wish to volunteer by campaigning for an office with a service club, working with the Food Bank or helping with the homeless. Consider expanding your favorite hobbies or beginning a new one such as painting or weaving. Supplementing your income through commercializing a hobby, starting a new business, or working part time, all need to be factored into your retirement plans. Can you and your partner handle being together 24/7?

Both spouses or partners need to do this exercise, to identify any major disagreements before you make the retirement leap. A sound relationship can be torn apart when you and your partner cannot agree on your retirement lifestyle. One of you may wish to travel, while the other has traveled extensively during his or her career, and now only wishes to be a home body. Another challenge is when one of you has been at home long enough to establish a major circle of friends, which did not include your spouse or partner. Or, you have an extensive circle of friends in your work-a-day world, with few friends outside of work. A general agreement about how your differing activities will be balanced within your retirement lifestyle is a must, or retirement may be more stressful than working full time.

Chapter One

At age 79 and 15 years of a productive and wonderful retirement, I want to share some ideas and retirement secrets. Hopefully, the experiences of my wife and I will give you a starting point for designing your own successful retirement program.

The following are some mind joggers to help you get your retirement plan started. Some of the questions you need to answer are:

- ☆ When do I want to retire?
- ☆ When can I retire?
- ☆ How do I do it?
- ☆ What do I need?
- ☆ How can I get ready?
- ☆ Do I have enough money?

Knowing the correct answers to the above questions is a must. This is a "Do not kid ourselves time." It is imperative to thoroughly analyze your cash flow to judge the potential success of your retirement decision. Most of you will still require at least 70% to 80% of your present income to maintain your current lifestyle during retirement. Many fall into the trap of thinking their cost of living will be cut in half when retired. It seldom happens.

The sad fact is that you tend to devote more time researching a two week trip to Rome than analyzing your retirement options and finances. Remember, you are committed to these decisions for the next 30 or 40 years. You must recognize, once you quit your current job, seldom can you regain that job or achieve that level of income again. You should consider retirement as a 30+ year period of unemployment and plan accordingly.

Determining your current cost of living and cash flow is one of the more time consuming exercises you need to do when planning your retirement. You must determine how much money you need each month to maintain your lifestyle. Your expense analysis may involve reviewing your canceled checks, automatic payment accounts, credit card invoices, plus your cash outlays, to learn where you are today. Your most recent income tax report can provide considerable data, particularly on the income side of the ledger. This is a very critical step to a successful retirement, so don't skip over it.

Once you accumulate your income and expense figures, many free retirement analysis programs are available for additional refinement. Visit my website, www.jimrolson.com, for these resources and websites. You will find links to Fidelity, MSN, Vanguard, among others. In addition, my site's resource section also provides **Expense and Cash Flow Worksheets** to assist projecting your retirement finances. These sites will help you learn how to adjust your own personal finances in order to maintain your desired lifestyle.

If your projected income in retirement is less than the desired 70 to 80% of your current income, then adjustments must be made. Reducing your expenses or increasing your income are two of the possible alternatives available. This book will give you a number of options for enjoying your retirement, even if your retirement income is less than 70% of your current income. More of the financial side of retirement will be explored in Chapters Four and Five.

When we first retire, it may seem like an extended vacation. But you will soon discover, playing golf, sunbathing on the beach, or lounging on your patio become boring if this is all there is. My goal in this book is to help you make your retirement affordable, interesting and fun. When properly planned, retirement can mean jumping out of bed each morning, excited to see what new adventures today will bring.

Chapter Two

Where to Retire?

One of the most basic questions anyone considering retirement must ask is, "Where do I want to live in retirement?" The options are tremendous, including:

☆ Your existing home;
☆ Another location in your same community;
☆ The Sunbelt;
☆ A Retirement Community;
☆ Overseas;
☆ A Recreational Vehicle;
☆ Or anywhere it makes sense to you.

Initially, the easiest decision is to stay where you are. If your current location works for you, stay put, giving you time to weigh some of the above options. You have many years of retirement ahead of you, so don't rush your decisions. Ideally, wait at least one year before making a major relocation. The main risk of purchasing a different property is, that in a normal real estate market, it will require three to five years before you can resell it at a high enough price to cover all of your costs. Typically, the selling costs of your property will average about 10 percent of the sales price. The selling costs must cover commission, transaction taxes, plus escrow and title insurance fees.

In a normal real estate market, residential property only appreciates at about the rate of inflation. The crazy real estate market between 2005 and 2008, with its doubling in price every six months to a year, was an aberration. The harm this wild market did to the world's economy will leave scars that may take decades to heal. Financial and governmental institutions will tighten their standards to protect against a repeat of the mistakes of the first decade of the 21st century. **Be conservative in retirement.**

Elimination of mortgage payments should always be a top priority within retirement. If you enjoy your current community, consider downsizing, by selling your existing, larger home. Replace it with a smaller, more manageable dwelling. Easier and less costly maintenance, plus elimination of stairs, are great benefits. Hips and knees can become more than a little annoyance when surgery requires crutches and walkers. Also, you can generate a nice increase in your liquid assets by reducing your dollars committed to housing.

Many times a recreational property, such as your weekend waterfront cabin, rural acreage or a snowbird condo, you already own, becomes the ideal retirement home. If you still owe on it, sell your primary home and pay off the recreational property mortgage. Then, relocate to your recreational community where you probably already have many friends.

Most often, the recreational home is in a rural area, so there are several things to consider. Medical care is many times a volunteer EMT, or Emergency Medical Technician, who will provide advanced first aid, but little more. The fire department may be volunteers, who must be called out from their homes whenever a fire occurs. Seldom will they reach your home in time to save it, rather, they will only be able to save your neighbor's property. Typically, hospitals are 30 to 50 miles away.

These are only minor inconveniences when you just spend weekends and vacations, but when you are full time, they can become major considerations.

When moving to your recreational property, plan ahead to when you will move back to the city. Aging in a rural place is a nice concept, but health care and proximity to your kids, grandkids and a super market create strong pulls back to town. Your doctor, dentist, a good hospital, the theater, shopping and convenient services, are the other side of the coin from rural living. My wife and I have lived many years in both settings, and we found rural living was perfect for the first 10 to 15 years in retirement, while urban convenience and security won out later in life.

Retirement may bring out your nomad spirit, and a life on the road in an RV could suit your lifestyle goals. You may dream of selling your home and buying a deluxe motor home or a diesel pickup and large, roomy, 5th wheel trailer. Before spending large amounts for an RV, consider renting or buying an older unit, which can be disposed of without a large loss. It's better to hold off on your commitment to full time RV'ing until you research it fully.

Before selling your primary home, hit the road to try out your wandering spirit. Whether you head for the Arizona or California deserts in the winter, or into Canada or Alaska in the summer, you will meet many wonderful, like-minded people. There will be many opportunities to have a toddy with your RV park neighbor, where you can learn the pros and cons of RV living. RV park space costs $20 to $40 per day, and this can become a major expense. A campground membership could be your answer.

Many times you can acquire a $3000 campground membership for $1000 to $1500, if you buy direct from an existing member. For a fee of around $250 per year, you can stay free, two weeks at a time, at any of your program's associated RV parks. For as little as an additional

$129 per year, you can double the number of available parks by joining an affiliated RV group. Western Horizons, AOL, 1000 Trails, Resorts of Distinction, Coast to Coast and Good Sam are just a few groups available. Most are listed on the internet, and my website includes links to many of them. Be alert to your RV neighbors, for they may be interested in selling their membership. Also, RV magazines, Craig's List or your local newspaper may have ads for memberships at meaningful discounts.

We spent the first four months of our retirement in our 5th wheel at our Western Horizons home park in St. George, Utah. My wife attended quilting classes, I enrolled in a 10 week golf program for seniors, plus we toured much of southwestern Utah. Also, we were only two hours north of Las Vegas and 45 minutes from Mesquite, Nevada. We saw shows, a little gambling and really enjoyed ourselves. The only problem was, it had become just an extended vacation, and we missed home. We were glad to have tried RV living, but we found it was still just a recreation for us. For someone else, it could be the perfect life style. Try it, you might like it.

As a Snow Bird, with your permanent dwelling in your old community, plus a condo or RV space in the Sunbelt, you have the best of both worlds. You retain your original friends and acquaintances, plus acquire a whole new set of friends in Arizona, Palm Springs, Florida or wherever. Your experimental travels, checking out the RV life, are great times to search for Snow Bird locations. Visit RV style parks, Park Model trailers or condos to see what fits your lifestyle and budget. A reverse approach might be to live in the Sunbelt during winter, with a waterfront cottage or live-aboard boat in the north during summer.

Down-sizing your primary home can help keep your costs manageable when owning multiple locations. Something to think about, both dwellings need someone to look after them while you are away. A Home Owner's Association, gated community or friendly neighbors or relatives, willing to keep an eye on your place while you are gone, helps with your peace of mind. A private hideaway in a rural setting is wonderful when you are there, but someone could load everything into a moving van while you are gone and no one would know.

A viable option, particularly for a single person, is to move back home with your kids. This requires careful consideration for it to work perfectly. If a portion of your youngster's home is available to convert to an independent apartment, it can be ideal. If both parties maintain the two households as completely separate dwellings, it really helps. Agreeing that no one visits or walks into the other dwelling without calling first is a good rule. If there are still grandkids at home, have an understanding about how much free babysitting is expected of you. Also, agreeing on how expenses will be divided is a must.

A new concept appearing in many communities is a special zoning change, allowing a mother-in-law cottage or studio on the same lot as the single family dwelling. Prefabricated, standalone studio or one bedroom units are available in some communities. They are complete with plumbing, appliances and ready to move in. In the Greater Seattle area, the costs vary from $70,000 to $100,000. Check with your local Home Builders Association for availability in your area. In addition, contact your city or county building department to check the zoning ordinances to see what is permitted in the area you wish to occupy.

Some of you more adventuresome types have vacationed around the world. You have found areas where you could live a fairly pampered life, with gardeners, housekeepers and cooks, for less than your regular costs in the United States. Whether Mexico, Costa Rica, Belize or the Mediterranean, it makes for exciting dreams. You must adapt to many new factors, such as, language, health care, how the natives feel about "foreigners", plus, noncitizen property ownership. Also, consider currency differences, job availability, U.S. pension access, driver's license and how to bring your car with you. An excellent reference source on the internet is www.ExpatExchange.com. They have a newsletter and can help you learn the important considerations for living most anywhere in the World. My website, www.jimrolson.com, has the Expat link and added info.

Be sure you take advantage of the freedom retirement allows. Many of us just assume we will stay in our existing home and travel, garden or visit the kids and grandkids. Do some real brainstorming to identify the exciting lifestyle changes which may now be available to you. You may only have this opportunity once in life, so consider adding some major changes to your "Bucket List".

As you read on in this book, you will encounter many of the available lifestyle opportunities, including:

Having More Fun:
- ☆ Affordable worldwide travel
- ☆ Family togetherness at home
- ☆ New and expanded hobbies
- ☆ Significant time with kids and grandkids
- ☆ Youth mentoring

Making a Profit:
- ☆ Converting a hobby to a business
- ☆ Consulting
- ☆ Board of Directors positions
- ☆ Full time Investor
- ☆ Teaching
- ☆ New Career

Chapter Three

A Hut or a Mansion?

Remaining in your existing home when retired tends to be the first choice for many, because no major effort or decisions are required. Your property may be free and clear or have a small mortgage, and you are comfortable with the structure. But, staying in your existing home may not be your best choice in the long run. You need to accept that in most cases your existing home is sized for a family, with three to five bedrooms, and is not designed for empty-nesters to age in place.

A lot of homes have stairs, with bedrooms upstairs and the laundry in the basement. Also, four to six steps up to your front or back door are common. A wheelchair ramp into your home requires one foot laterally for each one inch rise, so not every home can successfully add a ramp. When the inevitable knee or hip surgery occurs, or debilitating health problems rear their ugly head, the stairs become your enemy. Sleeping on the living room sofa, because you can't safely manage crutches up and down the stairs, gets old in a hurry. Homes built 20 or more years ago usually have some narrow doors, such as into the bathroom, which are only 30 to 32 inches wide. If you are confined to a wheel chair, even temporarily, a comfortable lifestyle may be nearly impossible. Even getting in and out of a bathtub can be an enormous problem for anyone who is physically challenged.

One option is to have an architect, knowledgeable in senior housing design, give you an estimate for the cost to convert your home to a dwelling suitable for aging in place. This information will help you determine the cost vs. benefit of remodeling your present home or relocating to a more age friendly dwelling. If, like most retirees, you are in good health, the design limitations of your existing home will not be an immediate problem. But, at some point, you will need to face the limitations of your current design, and either remodel or move.

Big changes should be controlled by you, in your time frame, and not when something or somebody else forces you to change. With the aging population of Boomers, more developers are building age friendly housing. Two bedroom, two bath homes, with no stairs, 36 inch doors throughout, no step-over showers or walk-in tubs, easy opening door handles, garage access into the kitchen and minimal care landscaping, are becoming available. Downsizing from your large family home, and moving to a new, age friendly home or a condo, can make your aging in place much more realistic. No one likes to move, as it can be a stressful occurrence, but your benefits may far outweigh the costs and stress of your staying put.

Full time RV'ing is a viable option for some, but as we discussed earlier, be certain you are ready for this change in lifestyle. RV's tend to lose up to one third of their value the day you drive them off of the lot, so buying a nearly new, used rig can be your best way to go. A surprising number of people buy expensive new RV's, only to discover they miss their kids and grandkids too much to stay on the road. Or, one of the couple develops a health issue, and they are forced to sell their almost new unit. Buying one of these rigs may save you many thousands of dollars, with minimal risks. Seniors tend to take excellent care of their units, so buying one from them is normally a pretty safe bet. A lot of the rigs are still under a transferrable factory warranty, protecting you from unexpected repair costs.

Visiting RV shows and searching the dealer lots will provide a solid education, and will help you learn what is available and the typical costs. Plus, this type of research is great recreation, particularly if you leave your check book home.

Whether to buy a motor home, truck and 5th wheel or a travel trailer is debated, ad infinitum, around the campfires. The general opinion seems to be, **the motor home is more fun while you are traveling, while the trailer is the best choice for comfort after you get there.** If you are mainly touring the North American continent, the motor home and suitable towed vehicle are the way to go.

Many new RV'ers plan to tow an existing car behind their motor home. One caution, only certain cars can be towed without modification to keep their transmissions from overheating. Most RV dealers know which towed vehicles work the best. Also, a modification will be required so the brakes of the towed vehicle will be activated by the motor home brakes.

Travel trailers and 5th wheel trailers, with three to four slide-outs, fireplaces, large flat screen TV's, washer/dryers and king or queen sized beds, have become more common. You are not sacrificing comfort with these units. You may hesitate to own a 5th wheel or trailer due to concerns that you can't successfully back these units. But, this isn't as big a problem as you might imagine. Most RV parks have pull through sites, eliminating need to back. Backing a trailer is a learned skill, which, with practice, you can soon accomplish. A 5th wheel is a little easier to handle than a travel trailer, for it overlaps your truck bed by about four feet. This shortens your overall length, and eliminates much of the side sway as you drive down the highway. If your tow vehicle is a Suburban style, or a pickup and canopy, a travel trailer is the only way to go. There are anti-sway hitches and special vehicle suspension systems to eliminate the highway handling problems associated with some travel trailers.

Buying new equipment will cost from $100,000 to $140,000 for a heavy duty diesel truck and a 34 to 38 foot fifth wheel trailer. A comparable setup, one or two years old, will cost from $60,000 to $100,000. The pull vehicle becomes your mode of transportation once you arrive at your destination. A new 36 to 40 foot diesel pusher motor home will cost between $200,000 and $400,000, depending on the quality and options. Similar, nearly new units are available for $125,000 to $250,000. The towed vehicle and car towing dolly, if needed, will add to the cost.

The debate between diesel and gas powered units goes on and on. New diesel pusher motor homes, with the engine in the rear, may cost $75,000 to $100,000 more than a comparably sized gas powered unit. The diesel longevity of around 300,000 miles, compared to 100,000 for a gas motor home engine, is one of the major reasons for the difference in cost. Another factor, the size of the gas powered Class A units usually are less than the diesel pushers. The bigger gas Class A rigs typically top out at 34 to 35 feet, whereas the diesels can be up to 45 feet in length. The diesels have terrific power and torque, using large commercial type truck engines, coupled to special six-speed automatic transmissions to handle the extra weight. While a large gas powered motor home may get seven to eight miles per gallon on the freeway, the diesel rigs may get eight to ten or eleven miles per gallon. The diesels will out-pull most any gas rig climbing the high passes of the Rockies. A used gas powered unit may sell for 25 to 35% less than the comparable diesel rig.

A buyer must weigh the power, long life and pride of ownership of a diesel versus the affordability of a gas unit. The best answer to the debate is to find a dealer, whose judgment you trust, and draw from his or her experience.

Downsizing from your home to a manufactured home park for age 55 and older can prevent or eliminate many cash flow challenges. You can find modern, 2 or 3 bedroom, 2 bath homes, ranging from 1500 to 1800 square feet, for only $35,000 to $75,000. The monthly park fees, including most utilities, except power, average $400 to $500 per month.

Generally, senior manufactured home parks have controlled access and good security. With the age and restrictive covenants, you will not be faced with derelict cars, boats or ATV's in your neighbor's driveway.

Even if you don't currently own a home with equity, a 55 and older manufactured home park may still be worth considering. Your total monthly living expense may be considerably less than renting. It is certainly worth doing a direct comparison between your current costs versus living in a seniors' park. Owning only the dwelling for $50,000 and not the land, may make ownership affordable, compared to $250,000 to $400,000 for a typical home. Another factor relates to traveling or snow-birding, allowing you to leave your personal effects in a secure home when you are gone for extended periods.

The modern, seniors only parks, are a major upgrade from the days of Tobacco Road, with many professional and highly educated residents. A retired professor, a ballet and tap dance instructor, still teaching, and an owner of a commercial janitorial firm, are typical resident-owners in local manufactured home parks.

Creating liquidity by selling your large family sized home, and moving to a 55 and older park, can provide the funds to become a snowbird. A Sunbelt condo or an owned or leased RV site can be a perfect match to a manufactured home park dwelling. Your current home equity will likely enable owning both properties free and clear, which is ideal. The daily security found in these types of properties gives you complete peace of mind when you are away for extended periods.

You may have heard of mobile homes, manufactured homes and modular homes, but were never quite certain of the difference. Mobile homes and manufactured homes are basically synonymous, but the units are so large that they are not very mobile, once in place. They now use 2 by 6 inch walls, and meet most of the national building codes. They can be a real value, with the cost per square foot of living space as little as 50% of a similar sized, site built home. The manufactured or mobile home has two long steel I-beams running the length of each unit, with two or three axles. The manufactured homes travel to their end site on their own wheels. Technically, they do not require a perimeter foundation, with the long I-beams supported by special pier blocks.

A modular home may look the same as a regular manufactured home, but they are delivered to the building site on flatbed trailers, without I-beams. Then, they slide the two or three, fourteen foot wide units onto a prebuilt, cement foundation. Banks normally use the same lending and interest rate standards for modular as they do for regular homes built on site. Lenders may shorten the loan period or charge higher rates for manufactured homes than loans for modular homes. This is especially true if the units are going to a park, where you do not own the land. You should check with the lenders and insurance companies prior to committing to a manufactured home to be certain suitable loan packages and rates are available. Many manufactured home dealers are also producing modular homes for only about $10.00 per square foot more than a mobile home.

If you are not quite ready for the higher densities, which occur in manufactured home parks, a manufactured home or modular on owned real estate is a viable option. Manufactured homes in a park tend to depreciate, similar to an automobile. **Located on owned real estate, new units tend to hold their initial value, and don't depreciate like they do in a park.** In a normal real estate market, which we may not see for a few more years, both the modular and site built dwelling and the land will appreciate together. Whereas, a manufactured home on real estate will just hold its value, with only the land appreciating. Some city zoning does not allow manufactured housing, so check with your planning department before purchasing.

If you are a boater or a boat owner wanna-be, another alternative living style is available. Summer cruising the East Coast Inland Waterway, the Inside Passage to Alaska, the Great Lakes or the Caribbean, can be a dream come true. Then haul out for the winter and head for a condo in Florida or the desert Sunbelt of Arizona, California or Texas. In the Pacific Northwest a forty foot power or sailboat can provide comfortable year around living. A solid used boat can be purchased for $1500 to $2000 per lineal foot. The icing on the cake is, summers in the U.S. San Juan Islands or north into the Canadian Gulf Islands or Southeastern Alaska, can be spectacular. People pay $1,000's to experience what you can enjoy for basically the cost of your fuel. If you happen to own a sailboat, even the costs of fuel are minimal. Year around moorage is available for around $200 to $400 per month on Lake Washington or Lake Union, adjacent to Puget Sound, or on Puget Sound itself.

When my wife and I sold our real estate business, we were faced with lifestyle decisions, like most other new retirees. We owned a very private 3000 square foot log home, with 200 feet of salt water frontage, three acres of timbered uplands and a Japanese garden, plus two acres of clams and oysters. We now had the time to travel, but the risks of leaving our home unattended caused us to seek more secure alternatives.

We learned of "Panorama", a continuing care retirement community, in Lacey, Washington, about 60 miles south of Seattle. After several visits to Panorama, we could see the benefits of the natural setting without all of the work needed for us to maintain it. About a year and one half later, in June of 1999, we made the big move. We have never regretted the relocation to "Panorama", and we easily adjusted to being constantly pampered with all of the services. Worry free travel has been an added benefit. My website at www.jimrolson.com has links to access additional information and pictures of Panorama.

Continuing care is the designation for a community providing all levels of your senior living, from an independent home or apartment, progressing to a 24/7, skilled nursing facility. Most continuing care retirement communities or CCRC's, are designed to allow you to age in place, without ever leaving your community and friends. Panorama's dwellings vary from 1500 to 1800 square foot, two bedroom, two bath, lake front homes, to one and two bedroom ground level, garden court units, plus regular apartments. In addition, there are 50 one bedroom apartments for assisted living and a brand new, 155 bed skilled nursing complex.

The beautifully landscaped campus, including 100 foot tall fir trees, rhododendrons, azaleas and numerous evergreens, is like living in an arboretum. One bedroom garden court duplex and fourplex units cost $115,000, with two bedroom, two bath units costing $140,000 to $150,000. One bedroom apartments, with full kitchen, are priced from $80,000 to $115,000. Deluxe, 1600 square foot, two bedroom, two bath, view apartments are about $175,000. Standalone units with 1500 to 1800 square feet cost from $175,000 to $350,000, depending on location and features. Amenities, other than the landscaping, include an Aquatic and Fitness Center, with two pools and two equipment exercise rooms, a new 206 seat theater style auditorium and a brand new 155 bed Convalescent and Rehabilitation and skilled nursing facility. The skilled nursing facility includes an equipped 3000 square foot physical therapy gym.

Monthly costs vary from about $1100 to $1900 per month for a couple, depending on the size and location of their dwelling. Meals are available, but you are not required to pay for them as a part of your residency. The monthly bill includes all of your basic living expense, except your long distance calls and groceries. Your heat, light, basic telephone, cable TV, all maintenance, in and out, lawn and garden care and uniformed security are all included. There is also an RV storage lot with power, plus 125 free garden plots. The RV sites cost $25 per year, which pays the cost of someone mowing the grass. The garden plots are free.

Many of the residents travel extensively or snow bird for four to six months each winter. They let the management know when they are leaving and when they will return and also, if anyone has permission to enter the home in their absence. This starts a uniformed security employee inspecting the outside of their home at least daily, while the resident is gone. Security checks for unlocked doors and windows, and looks for anything out the ordinary. If they find a door or window unlocked, they will enter the home to check for any problems, and a written report will be left for management and the resident. Knowing their home is secure allows the resident to truly enjoy their time away.

There are numerous continuing care retirement communities across the United States and Canada, and their standards and services vary greatly. An excellent resource to check the strength and viability of CCRC's, in your region of interest, is CARF International and CARF-CCAC. CARF is an acronym for Commission Accreditation of Rehabilitation Facilities, while the related CCAC stands for Continuing Care Accreditation Commission. CARF is headquartered in Washington, DC, with offices in Tucson, AZ, and Edmonton, Alberta, Canada. They do an onsite accreditation of each of their members every one to five years. They check financial strength, along with the quality and extent of all services provided by the member CCRC reviewed. Do take advantage of CARF's information before committing your housing dollars to a Continuing Care Retirement Community. My website has more info.

Plan ahead, not for just next year, but for the next 15 years and beyond. Your time and effort spent determining the most suitable dwelling and location for your retirement lifestyle can pay many future dividends. Making tough decisions now can enhance the pleasures of your retirement. Retirement may be the longest phase of your life, so do it right. The next chapter will explore ways to be certain you have adequate finances to retire with your desired lifestyle.

Chapter Four

Are Your Finances Ready?

You have decided to retire, but you must determine when. It may be next month or 15 years from now, depending on how your finances work out. Now is the time you need to do some serious planning, because **retirement is really 30 plus years of unemployment.** Your finances must accommodate all of your needs over this extended period when recessions, stock market crashes, high inflation or personal catastrophes can occur.

One approach is to develop your retirement plan as if you were starting a new business. Your business plan must include all of the expenses you can identify, as well as a realistic estimate of your retirement income. You must recognize there is one major difference between a failed business plan and a failed personal retirement plan. The worst thing that can happen if your business fails, you may go bankrupt and have to start over. **If you underestimate your retirement financial needs, you may face poverty for the rest of your life.**

Your failure to live a productive and financially secure retirement should not be an option. This chapter will help you approach this most important step in your life in a logical and achievable manner. The chapter will provide examples of successful retirements, along

Retirement Expense Worksheet - Monthly		
	Expense Category	**Monthly Total**
Housing	Mortgage/Rent	$_____
	Property Tax	$_____
	Homeowner's Ins.	$_____
	Utilities	$_____
	Maintenance/Fees	$_____
Food	Groceries	$_____
	Dining Out	$_____
Transportation	Payments	$_____
	Fuel/Maintenance	$_____
	Public Transportation	$_____
Health Care	Medical Services	$_____
	Drugs/Supplies	$_____
	Health Insurance	$_____
Personal Insurance	Life Insurance	$_____
	Long Term Care	$_____
	Other Insurance	$_____
Personal Care	Clothing	$_____
	Products & Services	$_____
Family Care	Alimony	$_____
	Kids' Support	$_____
Miscellaneous	Loans/Credit Cards	$_____
	Entertainment	$_____
	Hobbies	$_____
	Travel/Vacation	$_____
	Gifts/Charitable Contrabu.	$_____
	Education	$_____
	Other	$_____
	Income Tax	$_____
Total Monthly Expenses		$_____

with tools to help you develop your own personal retirement plan. As everyone has unique financial requirements and income sources, there are a variety of concepts available. Let's review several approaches to successful retirement to see which ones fit your desired lifestyle. **Judge carefully how each of the retirement programs will work for you, and if in doubt, take the conservative approach.**

Now is the time for you and your spouse to take the time to document your current expenses, without assuming you can reduce your cost of living in retirement. Your check register, credit card statement, and, hopefully, a personal accounting program, such as Intuit's Quicken, will provide most of your data. The following is a simple summary format used by Vanguard that can get you started

Inflation must be recognized in your calculations for a successful retirement. We have all seen the disclaimer that, "past results are no assurance they will happen again in the future." This may be true for many investments, but inflation doesn't follow the rule. Since the early 1920's, inflation has averaged three percent increase annually, and since 1960, it has averaged nearly four percent.

The tendency of our politicians to throw money at problems, whether we can afford the solutions or not, will likely keep inflations climbing throughout your lifetime. The Rule of 72 estimates the years it takes a current dollar amount to double, when 72 is divided by the annual percentage rate of change. If the economy continues at the prewar rate of four percent per annum, all of your living costs will double in 18 years, or well within your lifetime.

Now one of the more important determinations is required. What retirement income will I need to cover my estimated expenses? Summarize your potential income sources, such as, Social Security, pension, investments and wages, if you plan to work in retirement, plus any other income.

Retirement Income Worksheet - Monthly Income		
Estimated Monthly Income		
Social Security	You	$_____
	Your Spouse	$_____
Wages	You	$_____
	Your Spouse	$_____
Pensions	You	$_____
	Your Spouse	$_____
Other Income	Rental Income	$_____
	Veteran's Benefits	$_____
	Investment	$_____
Total before Taxes		$_____
Estimated Tax Liability		
Federal Income Tax		$_____
State Income Tax		$_____
Local Income Taxes		$_____
Total After Tax Income		$_____
Deduct Total Expenses		$_____
Surplus or Shortfall		$_____

Now that you have identified your expenses and income in retirement, and you have determined any shortfall between the two, a plan to make up for any difference is your next step. Income from your nest egg assets may be the place for you to begin. Your real challenge is how you can generate enough funds to cover any income shortfall, and still make your nest egg last throughout your 30 plus years in retirement?

One often stated rule of thumb is to withdraw a dollar amount equal to four percent of your nest egg during the first year of retirement. Then withdraw the initial dollar amount, plus inflation, in subsequent years. This approach carries several serious risks. If the stock market declines in the first few years of retirement, your dollar withdrawal amounts will deplete your savings too quickly to support your entire retirement life span. Also, the system does not allow for unusual costs, such as health care demands, or an estate for your heirs.

A safer approach to annual withdrawals from your investments would be a set percentage, such as three to five percent of your nest egg. No adjustment is made for inflation, with the total dollar withdrawals varying each year, based upon the total of your investments. **You must be a good money manager to make this work.** In down years, lower your expenditures to use just the reduced dollar amount withdrawn. In good years, your withdrawal can increase, but don't spend it all. The best approach is to reinvest the excess above your normal living costs, or reduce the percentage you will withdraw. This will help you to maintain your standard of living in the down years.

Remember, **your cost of living will likely double within your lifetime.** Before you actually retire is the best time to design an investment program to handle this doubling of your living expenses. Plus, build an emergency fund for unexpected demands. You might think of this important step as your **Cash Flow for Life Plan.**

Here is an example for Bob and Sue, where Bob who will be age 64 as of January 1, 2012, and has an income of $65,000 per year. Sue will be 62, also January 1, 2012, and earns $35,000 per year. They have been considering a once in a lifetime birthday and retirement party on January 1, 2012, but as they do their income and expense research, some adjustments may be required. Their nest egg as of 1-1-2012 is estimated at:

Joint Taxable Acct.	$200,000
Bob's IRA	200,000
Sue's IRA	100,000
Bob's Roth IRA	100,000
Sue's Roth IRA	50,000
Total	**$650,000**

Estimated Annual Retirement Expenses: Bob & Sue	
Housing	$ 24,000
Payments, rent, taxes, utilities	
Food	$ 8,400
Groceries & dining out	
Auto & Transportation	$ 3,600
Pmts., fuel/maintenance, public trans.	
Health Care	$ 14,400
Medical, drugs/supplies, insurance	
Personal Insurance	$ 11,500
Life, long term care, other	
Family Care	$ 6,000
Alimony, adult kids	
Miscellaneous	$ 18,000
Income tax, credit cards/loans, travel, hobbies, entertainment	
Total Annual Expenses	$ 85,200
Income Before Tax	$ 75,000
Shortfall or Surplus	$ (10,000)

Estimated Annual Retirement Income - Bob & Sue		
Social Security	You	$ 16,850
	Your Spouse	$ 9,700
Pensions	You	$ 12,450
	Your Spouse	$
Wages	You	$
	Your Spouse	$
Other Income	Rental Income	$
	Veterans Benefits	$
	Investment & Miscellaneous	$ 36,000
Total Before Income Tax		$ 75,000

Estimated Tax Liability	
Federal Income Tax	$ 8,800
State Income Tax	$
Local Taxes	$
Total After Income Tax	$ 66,200
Deduct Total Expenses	$ 85,200
Surplus or Shortfall	$ (19,000)

Bob and Sue now face major decisions, for, although they both worked diligently and saved consistently, their retirement income is $19,000 less than the estimated annual retirement expenses. To maintain their desired standard of living in retirement, changes are required, with either more income or less expenses.

One viable solution to make up the shortfall would be to work an additional year, living on your $85,000 per year retirement budget. The $15,000 per year reduction in spending could be added to your normal $10,000 per year retirement savings, giving you an additional $25,000 added to your nest egg. Other steps are also needed to safely make up the $19,000 annual shortfall.

Social Security benefits provide one of your best returns when you delay retirement. From the initial age 62 to the maximum at age 70, for each year you delay receiving your benefits, you will increase your receipts by approximately eight percent. This certainly beats most safe investments. Bob and Sue's combined Social Security benefits would climb from $26,550 as of 1-1-2012, to approximately $29,060 as of 1-1-2013.

Another lifestyle change to insure adequate income for retirement could be to down-size your home. Bob and Sue, for instance, have a 4 bedroom, 2.5 bath home, purchased 20 years ago for $250,000. The original $50,000 down payment left a $200,000 mortgage, with payments of $1200 per month, including interest at 6%. Bob and Sue still owe $108,000 on their mortgage. During the real estate bubble, the home value was estimated at $500,000, but now it has dropped 20%, to $400,000.

They could consider selling their home for $400,000, receiving a net of approximately $250,000. This is after paying off their $108,000 mortgage, and the normal 10% home selling costs, including commissions, title insurance and escrow fees, plus local transaction taxes. In many markets, Bob and Sue could pay cash for a nice 2 bedroom, 2 bath condo for around $200,000, with $50,000 left over. The $650,000 nest egg would have grown by 5%, to $682,500, by delaying retirement one year. Then, adding the $50,000 from the downsizing of their home, plus the extra $25,000 of retirement savings, will give Bob and Sue a total nest egg of $757,500 when they retire January 1 of 2013.

The savings of $1200 per month, without the mortgage payment, would drop their retirement expenses to $70,800, rather than $85,200. Bob and Sue's shortfall now is $29,250 or $2438 per month, which will be funded from their nest egg investment income and withdrawals. During the next 10 years, beginning with the $757,500, their nest egg, should grow to $908,675, even when withdrawing 4% each year. This is based upon their nest egg compounding at 6%, inflation increasing at 3% and Social Security remaining indexed to inflation.

Be flexible and imaginative, and you can find ways to retire, even when your assets and investments have dropped in value. You may have a recreational home to which you could move, if you sell your primary residence. Or, by netting $250,000 from the sale of your home, you could invest the $250,000 at 6% per annum, and use the $1250 per month income to rent a suitable apartment or condo. Another viable option to investigate is a Continuing Care Retirement Community, such as Panorama in the Olympia area of Washington State. Here, you can obtain a beautiful home or large duplex with your $200,000 to $250,000 proceeds from your home.

CARF or the Commission on Accreditation of Rehabilitation Facilities has information on the quality and availability of other CCRC's across the nation. My website includes internet addresses for Panorama and CARF.

Remember, other than selecting your spouse or lifetime partner, **nothing is more important than preplanning your retirement.** Only about one person in four of retirement age has done any serious planning. Start planning as soon as possible, so you will be one of the 25 percent who succeed and really enjoy retirement. Don't allow a bad day at the office or a run-in with your boss push you into retiring before you are ready. **Do your in-depth planning and homework first.**

Chapter Five

Managing Finances in Retirement

You have made the big plunge into retirement, where there is no real turning back. This chapter will walk you through some of the alternatives available to help your funds last as long as you do.

Let's see how Bob and Sue might handle their finances for a long and successful retirement. Remember they had to generate $29,250 of investment income the first year or $2438 per month, to help fund their retirement. With 3% inflation, their annual expenses could climb from $70,800 to $95,000 within 10 years. But a careful, conservative investment program can handle this. By delaying retirement one year, their original nest egg grew to $682,500, plus they added $75,000 of new savings, and eliminated a $1200 house payment.

Their 1-1-2013 nest egg consisted of:	
Bob's regular IRA	$210,000
Sue's regular IRA	105,000
Bob's Roth IRA	105,000
Sue's Roth IRA	52,500
Joint Taxable Funds	285,000
Total	**$757,500**

A caution at this point, for I will make some assumptions on how investments will perform in the future, based upon past performance. Remember, past performance is not always an accurate indicator of future results. My main approach is to invest in mutual funds and index funds, providing a diverse cross section of investments, with low management costs. Discuss your personal finances with your own investment advisor or have a "For Fee" advisor help you develop a suitable retirement investment program.

Bob and Sue have decided to follow my basic retirement principals, which are:

- ☆ Invest conservatively.
- ☆ Be diversified.
- ☆ Use low cost mutual and/or index funds.
- ☆ Withdraw capital from taxable funds first.
- ☆ Utilize Roth or tax free funds last.
- ☆ Allocate 15%-20% for emergencies.
- ☆ Fund your retirement to at least age 95.

Bob and Sue have selected the following types of investments for the first five years of their investment plan as follows:

Joint taxable funds	-	S&P 500 Index Fund
Both Regular IRA's	-	Mutual Fund of Multiple Funds
Both Roth IRA's	-	Growth & Income Fund

The 500 Index Fund I used began in 1976 and has averaged an annual return of 10.34%. The 500 index includes the major companies of the U.S., which account for over 75% of the U.S. Stock market's value. The expense ratio for managing the fund is .17% per year. Instead of the 10.34% return, Bob and Sue have projected a return of only 7% per year, so bad periods, such as 2002 through 2011, will not create a complete disaster for their finances.

All of their first year $2438 per month will be withdrawn from their Joint Taxable account invested in the S&P 500 Index fund. The withdrawal will be adjusted upward for the rate of inflation, increasing to $3800 per month in the 10th year, but never exceeding 5% of their total portfolio. Although they will have withdrawn approximately $343,800 from a beginning balance of $285,000, Bob and Sue will still have nearly $77,000 in their Joint Account at the end of 10 years, due to the 7% return from the S&P 500 Index Fund.

The $315,000 from their combined Regular IRA's will be invested within the Multiple Fund of Funds. It is a composite of 11 funds, with a balanced structure of stocks and bonds. The investments range from 60%-70% common stocks, 20%-30% bonds and 10%-20% in a short term bond fund. The management fee is .34% per year. From 1985 to September of 2011 the average return has been 9.5% per year. Again, Bob and Sue have chosen to use a conservative estimate of 6.7% per year return for their IRA accounts, which will grow tax deferred until withdrawn. The 6.7% average return should allow their IRA's to grow to $614,000 over the first 10 years.

The $157,500 of Roth IRA's will be invested in a Growth and Income Fund, which has an expense ratio of .28% per year. Since its inception in 1970, the fund has returned approximately 10.13% per year. It has a typical ratio of about 1/3 stocks and 2/3 investment grade bonds, with the stocks having mostly higher than average dividends. Bob and Sue, again, only use a conservative 7% as the projected annual return from the Growth & Income Fund. Even if the fund only gains 7% per year, they should have $316,000 in their Roth IRA's in 10 years. This type of fund fits nicely into their Roth IRA's because the dividends and interest payments will never be subject to income tax.

At the end of the first 10 years Bob and Sue's $757,500 nest egg has grown to about $1,000,000, even though they withdrew $2438 to $3800 per month, to keep up with 3% inflation. This illustrates the power of compound interest. Remember, **if you put yourself into this 10 year example, you still must plan for another 20 years or so beyond.**

I am not a certified financial planner nor a stock analyst. My thoughts and recommendations merely reflect my experience investing since the mid-1950's. Although, overall, I have done fairly well, I have had some major hits to my investments. My broker's advice had me invested over 90% in equities in October, 2007, and as you can imagine, my investments lost nearly 50% of their value over the next 6 to 9 months. In fact, had I followed Bob and Sue's retirement investment program, when mine peaked in October of 2007, my net worth today would be nearly 50% higher than it is.

Individual investors, picking their own stocks, have a poor record over the years. We tend to buy during the peak frenzies of the market and sell when the market is at its low point. The "Buy high, sell low" approach is not conducive to a solid, long-lasting retirement program. This leaves you with two main choices; pay a broker to manage your funds, or, have a self-directed portfolio. Broker management will cost, typically, one to two percent of your portfolio every year. In addition, there may be up to two percent fees for buying and selling your investments. These expenses make it very difficult for a broker managed portfolio to beat the overall market, without taking unacceptable risks.

Cost, diversification, performance and tax implications are some of the most important items for you to consider when choosing investments. You might seriously consider an approach similar to Bob and Sue, where you partially self-directed, by selecting the most suitable mutual funds and index funds. A proper selection of funds will provide the diversification and balance to meet the needs of your retirement program.. Your investments should allow you to sleep at night or travel away from home without undo worry.

Careful planning is your most important step before you take the final plunge into retirement. If you are like many potential retirees, you may not have even the modest savings of Bob and Sue. What then are your comfortable retirement options? Your 401k got clobbered in the great 2007-2009 recession and your small pension, along with you and your wife's social security only total $3500 per month. Your estimated retirement expenses will be $5,000 per month, and your savings only total about $200,000. What do you really want and expect during your retirement?

Different housing and a new neighborhood could be realistic alternatives. What to do when your home value has dropped from $300,000 to $200,000, or less, and a sale will only net about $75,000? Your mortgage payment is $1000 per month. If you must retire, or strongly wish to retire, now is the time for a serious discussion with your partner or spouse. If you both agree, a lifestyle change may be the best solution to your need to retire now.

Your home tends to be one of your most costly assets, so a change here is usually a good place to start. Take a serious look at modern senior's manufactured home developments in your community. You will likely find a comfortable 1400 to 1500 square foot, two bedroom, two bath home available for $75,000, or less. The home owner's association fee or space rent is $300 to $500 per month, including all utilities except power.

Moving to the senior's manufactured home may save you about $1000 per month. Now, how do you make up the other $500 per month shortfall? As luck would have it, the manufactured home park needs a part time assistant manager for three days per week for four hours each day. The approximate $500 per month salary would cover your final income shortfall, making your retirement a success. Try not to spend any of your $200,000 savings, but allow it to grow at approximately 7% per year. At the end of five years it will have grown to nearly $285,000, and within ten years it could easily reach $400,000. At that time, if you no longer wish to work or you have other expenses, you can start to draw on your nest egg.

Set aside a period at the beginning of each year to review and update your retirement program. To be certain your retirement finances continue to meet your requirements, please commit to this annual review. No one has a good track record predicting the economy more than one to five years into the future. Your retirement success may require doing much of the following:

- ☆ Use personal accounting program.
- ☆ Update your investment model allocation.
- ☆ Rebalance your investments annually.
- ☆ Prepare for special or unusual expenses.
- ☆ Adjust budget to meet inflation expectations.
- ☆ Cut spending when investment assets fall. Maintain the flexibility and discipline to spend less when your investment returns drop, while saving more when you have a better than expected year.

These examples of imaginative planning before you retire will give you some ideas that can ensure a happy and productive lifestyle in retirement. If you have a spouse or partner, be certain to include them in all of your financial planning and retirement goals. Without agreement of where you are and where you want to be, your retirement years may not be as pleasant as they should be. **Plan as a team.**

Chapter Six

You Control the Budget

How can you control your budget rather than your budget controlling you? Learning this lesson will do more than anything else to help you achieve a satisfying and affordable retirement lifestyle.

Retiring involves both a challenge and a risk. The challenge is you now have a fixed income to live on. **The risk is, if you don't allocate this income properly, you face poverty.** You likely know your income right to the penny, but your expenditures are another matter. Many individuals have the problem of running out of money before they run out of month. This is the same problem which causes a person making $100,000 per year to go broke. It's really quite easy, you just spend $110,000.

Before direct deposit payrolls and without computers and software, how did you handle your budgets and finances? **Envelope Budgeting** was the classic method. This technique began when workers were paid in cash, and had to learn to make the cash last until the next payday. A separate envelope was marked for each of their major expense categories, such as rent, groceries, clothing, car, insurance, etc. The exact amount of money allocated to each of the categories scheduled for that pay period was placed in the designated envelope. If $200 was allocated for groceries during the two week pay period, you paid cash as you went along. If your envelope was empty before the next pay period, you could not spend any more for that category.

You can now use sophisticated software to do your Envelope Accounting, but the principle is still the same. You can be much more specific, with many more sub-categories within each major expense area. A category, such as Car might include:

☆ Gas
☆ Payment
☆ Maintenance
☆ Insurance

Once you have established sub-categories within each of your major expense areas, current software will allow a specific budget allocation for each of the sub-categories. As you post your actual expenditures for each sub-category, most software can compare expenses to your budget. It will then let you know if there will be enough money in the envelope to pay your bills. A few of the important categories, with sub-categories, might include:

☆ **Housing** - Payments, rent, taxes, utilities.
☆ **Food** - Groceries & dining out.
☆ **Auto & Transportation** - Payments, fuel/maintenance, public transport.
☆ **Health Care** - Medical services, drugs/supplies, insurance.
☆ **Personal Insurance** - Life, long term care, other.
☆ **Family Care** - Alimony, adult children.
☆ **Miscellaneous** - Income tax, credit cards, loans, travel, hobbies, entertainment.

Once you establish the categories and sub-categories, as well as the budgeted amounts for each and their frequency, your financial life becomes much simpler. At the beginning of the month, the software provides a list of the payments needed during the month, along with their amounts. Infrequent payments, such as quarterly taxes, semi-annual property taxes, insurance payments, car licenses, etc., can all be included in your monthly budget schedule. Your financial life can now be efficiently handled with only three or four hours of effort per week.

You can program some of the accounting software to provide you with a complete personal finance package. The various reports available are only limited by the amount of data you provide to the accounting program.

Some of the more useful reports available to you are:

- ☆ **Banking** - Cash flow, check book reconciliation, & expenditures by list of transactions.
- ☆ **Comparison Accounting** - Your expenditures & income by category, compared to budget or prior periods.
- ☆ **Investing** - Capital gains, investment allocations, gains & losses, transactions & portfolio value.
- ☆ **Net Worth & Balances** - Provides net worth, plus account balances.
- ☆ **Spending** - Relates to comparison accounting.
- ☆ **Tax Accounting** - Capital gains, Schedule A-Itemized deductions, Schedule B, Schedule D-Investment capital gains and losses, Tax Schedule & Tax Summary.
- ☆ **Business Accounting** (If applicable) - Cash Flow, Profit & Loss, Balance Sheet & Schedule C data.

Your budgeting and personal accounting approach isn't nearly as important as your commitment to actually doing it. The approaches can vary from something as simple as a free Microsoft Budget Template, to something as sophisticated as **Intuit's Quick Books**. The internet or your local office supply store have all levels of budgeting and accounting tools. There is even a free **Expense Manager** application for your cell phone to help keep track of your finances. Remember, the risk of failure to handle your retirement finances properly is <u>**poverty**</u>!

Staying within your budget may require something in addition to a sophisticated accounting program. I'll touch on some budget techniques for you to consider, which may apply to your own finances. Here are a few tips to help you control your budget:

- ☆ **Put your money where it isn't easy to access.** Use direct payments for your retirement savings, your house and car payments, insurance and any other scheduled expenses which you can't miss. Resist the urge to delay critical payments.
- ☆ **Never shop without a list.** Prepare your grocery list or personal care needs at home, to avoid the risk of impulse buying.
- ☆ **Know your monthly income and expenses.** Keep track of your expenditures on a cell phone application or a pocket sized journal, and save all receipts. Keep each month's receipts in an envelope, which can help at Income Tax time. Don't cheat and forget to log your $5 mocha, etc. You are only fooling yourself. If you have too much month at the end of the money, your records will help you prioritize your spending. It might only involve buying a $150 espresso machine, which, at $5 per mocha, would pay for itself in less than 60 days. You could also pack your lunch four days per week, with eating out on Fridays. Small changes can fix your budget.
- ☆ **Expensive friends can blow your budget.** Friends belonging to the golf and country club, with season football tickets, or taking long, annual cruises, can wreck havoc with your finances. Don't try to emulate their lifestyle without adequate income. They may be living on credit or not saving for retirement to fund their lifestyle. It may be better to find a new circle of friends in order to live within your means.
- ☆ **Have a little cash each week for a special treat.** If you feel the budget is too restrictive, you tend to ignore it, so have a little fun.
- ☆ **The budget is your friend, don't fight it.** Be one of the 25% with a workable, detailed budget. Prioritize your savings and retirement expenses to allow your retirement when you want it, rather than having to wait.

Chapter Seven

Income-Timing-Lifestyle

I will cover added income and working in retirement within three sections, because **why and when you retire varies** so greatly. The need or wish to work after retirement is a very personal decision, and each of us must determine how working fits our desired lifestyle. Take the time to analyze your particular situation and what some of your important options might be.

Some questions you should consider are:

☆ Do you need more money for your lifestyle?
☆ How much additional income do you need?
☆ Are your health care benefits adequate?
☆ How does work income affect Social Security?
☆ Do you wish full or part time employment?
☆ How important is the social side of work?
☆ What are your strengths and weaknesses, i.e., education, work experience or hobbies.
☆ Stay in your existing community or move?
☆ How is your physical fitness and health?
☆ How does your spouse/partner feel about work?
☆ Will you be bored without working?
☆ Do you wish to pursue new interests?
☆ What jobs are available?

Answers to the above questions will vary greatly, depending on why and when you are retiring. Chapter 7 will guide you in handling the various options the answers to these questions provide. It will explore how you might react to three of the major categories for retirement, which many of you will face, such as:

- ☆ **Forced retirement** due to firm bankruptcy, job cutbacks or business liquidation and closure
- ☆ **Voluntary early retirement**
- ☆ **Normal retirement** at age 65 and above

FORCED RETIREMENT

In today's economy, many retirements are not voluntary. Firms may be laying off workers to improve profits, or some companies are closing their doors due to bankruptcy or lack of a buyer. An all too common example is an individual at only age 59 and not qualified for Social Security, nor eligible for Medicare, which begins at 65, and loses their job.

Let's use Sam and Martha as an example. Sam's firm closed and he lost his $58,000 per year sales engineer position. He retained only his $250,000 IRA savings, with no severance pay. Martha is an administrative assistant, earning $15 per hour. This is about $2600 per month, with take home pay of about $2100, before $250 retirement deductions. Between them they have a total retirement savings of $300,000. Both Sam and Martha were covered by health insurance with Sam's firm, but now they must both apply for coverage from Martha's company. The employees within Martha's firm pay one-third of their health care premium, which will cost a total of $500 per month for Sam and Martha.

Although the extra $500 per month is tough to meet, it's still less than the typical total cost of health care insurance for two persons of $1200 to $1500 per month. If you lose the group coverage from your ex-employer, **it's critical to find other group insurance within 60 days.** The main consideration is to find a group policy if at all possible, for the group rates usually are the best.

Chapter Seven

If you have a choice, be cautious before you jump into the early retirement mode and carefully weigh the consequences. Let's follow the challenges of Sam and Martha, when Sam's early forced retirement creates numerous financial problems. These problems are typical for many who are forced into or desire early retirement during these financially difficult times.

Sam and Martha's gross income was about $89,000 per year, with take home pay of around $72,000. They then allocated 16%, or $12,000, toward their IRA retirement nest egg. Sam was paying 75% or $9000 of the $12,000 per year, and Martha contributed the other $3000 into their IRA's. Sam, at 59, had planned to work until age 66, to receive full Social Security benefits. By funding their retirement account with $1000 per month, they would have had a nest egg of around $530,000. This assumes they would have continued to receive a 6.5% tax deferred return on their savings. Now, with only $300,000 in their retirement account, and no job for Sam, serious adjustments are required.

When Sam was working full time, with their combined take home pay of $60,000, after allocating $12,000 to savings, their $5,000 monthly budget was:

Monthly Budget	
Mortgage Payment	$1200
Real estate tax & maintenance	400
Food & dining out	800
2 cars, insurance & payments	700
Utilities	300
Medical and Dental expense	400
Misc- Inc. Tax, Cr. Cards, Travel, etc,	1200
Total	$5000

Anyone facing the challenges of Sam and Martha will need to make some adjustments to their lifestyle in order to have any hope for a comfortable 30 plus year retirement.

Don't make radical moves before you have reviewed all of your options. If Sam was in the State of Washington he could qualify for unemployment benefits of approximately 50% of his gross income for a period of 26 weeks. The Washington State Security Department has an online unemployment benefits calculator to help you estimate your benefits. They recommend you use the average of your 2 highest quarters of gross pay, during the first 4 of the last 5 quarters, prior to your filing for unemployment. They then multiply this average, which was $14,500, by the factor of .0385, to obtain the approximate weekly benefit amount. In Sam's case the weekly benefit estimate was $558 per week or a little over $2400 per month, which is 50% of his gross income.

The safest approach is to treat the internet unemployment income data as only an estimate. Each State in the U.S. has its own unemployment system, so the income you might receive will vary by your location. Once again, the internet is a great resource, but only a specialized government employee can give you the exact amounts and coverage periods. The specialist will instruct you as to your duties, such as job search and paperwork, necessary to continue qualification for your benefits.

Sam's approximate $2400 per month unemployment, along with Martha's approximate $2100 per month, after she stops the $250 per month she had been saving toward their retirement, still leaves them about $1000 per month short of meeting their current lifestyle expenses. How can they make ends meet while Sam searches for a suitable job to carry them through the next six or seven years to a more ideal retirement age? This is particularly difficult with the added $500 for insurance from Martha's firm, raising their budget to $5500 per month.

Although regular unemployment benefits continue for at least six months, don't delay actively looking for new employment.

Unfortunately, some people seem to treat unemployment benefits as if they were a vacation with pay. Please resist this temptation, because, during tough economic times, finding suitable work is difficult. Companies are very choosy and competition for the jobs is fierce. **Use every resource available.** Check with your college or university for career guidance or counseling. For example, the University of Washington, has career counseling sessions for as little as $60 per hour. They will help you analyze your strengths and weaknesses, plus guide you to the best opportunities within the current job market.

The internet can be a wonderful resource for getting your career back on track. Sites such as acinet.org/acinet/skills and aarp.org are just two of many excellent career guidance sites. They direct your focus to:

1. Your strengths and weaknesses
2. Available jobs
3. Resumes
4. How to apply and handle interviews

Not all online job help sites are ethical, so your caution is advised. Use only reputable firms. Your State Attorney General office can make you aware of firms with complaints or judgments against them. Your own personal network of friends and associates can also be of help.

Finding the right job may require the full six months of unemployment compensation, so how do Sam and Martha handle the $1000 dollar budget short fall? Sam, who is 59 1/2 years old, has about $250,000 in his IRA, which he can tap, without penalty. It may make sense to use some of Sam's and Martha's retirement savings to get by until Sam finds a suitable job. **Each person's tax situation is different, so check with your tax advisor or the IRS to learn how the laws apply to you.**

Let's review some of the more important Federal Income Tax laws which may apply to Sam's IRA:

4-Star Retirement 2-Star Budget

1. At age 59 1/2 you can withdraw any amount without penalty.
2. Withdrawals that were tax deferred, when deposited, will be taxed as regular income.
3. Age 50 and older, alright to save an extra $1000 per year, in addition to the normal $5000.
4. Funding and deductibility may be limited if you are covered by an employer retirement plan.
5. Income determines IRA eligibility.

Sam and Martha have worked hard and saved judiciously to build their retirement nest egg, and they don't wish to spend it now, before retirement. But, circumstances may dictate careful use of 5 to 10% of Sam's IRA to cover the $1000 budget shortfall during the job search. Withdrawing $1000 per month for a six month period can keep them from missing car or mortgage payments until Sam gets back on his feet. Withdrawing as much as $12,000 from Sam's $250,000 IRA should still allow it to grow back to $350,000 by Sam's 66th birthday, thanks to compound earnings of around 6.5% per annum.

Sam's job hunting efforts paid off and he was hired as a route driver in the food industry. Although his old job paid closer to $5000 per month, while the new position pays $4000, with careful lifestyle adjustments, a comfortable retirement is attainable. Sam and Martha's combined before tax income of $77,000 will provide approximately $69,000 after taxes. They can allocate $9000 per year to their retirement accounts and still manage their $60,000 per year budget. With Sam's old job, they saved $1000 per month. To meet their expenses, this new combined total for savings has to drop to $750 per month. This will still amount to a nest egg of about $490,000 in Sam's retirement in 6 years.

With Sam's old job, saving $1000 per month, they would have had $530,000 at retirement. Now with $40,000 less nest egg, they can either down scale a small amount or they can work a year longer before retiring. This is just one example how you can still manage a comfortable retirement, even when an apparent financial disaster hits.

VOLUNTARY EARLY RETIREMENT

Many of you have saved a fair sized nest egg and may wish to consider early retirement, which most consider as retiring before Medicare and full Social Security eligibility begin. You may need to consider a few lifestyle changes in order to meet the challenges of 30 years of retirement. I will help you review some of the benefits and cautions for successful early retirement. I'll emphasize some of the methods for supplementing your income during your retirement, to make your lifestyle even more fulfilling.

As you study your money needs to make retirement work, you may find a need for another $1000 to $2000 per month. Don't take this budget requirement as a failure to prepare for retirement. Rather, consider this an opportunity to extend your life. A number of studies have determined, working in retirement is good for your health, whether you need the money or not. Working in retirement is not unique. In fact, about 25% of total income reported for persons over age 65 is earned income.

In October, 2009 a group of researchers, from the University of Maryland, published a study in the *Journal of Occupational Health Psychology*, about working after retirement. They studied 12,189 participants, between the ages of 51 and 61, over a period of six years. Their findings determined that retirees who transition from full-time into a temporary or part-time job experience fewer major diseases and are able to function better day-to-day than people who stop working altogether. The researchers considered only physician diagnosed health problems, such as high blood pressure, diabetes, cancer, lung disease, heart disease, stroke and psychiatric problems.

Two of the co-authors, Mo Wang, PhD, and Kenneth Shultz, PhD, reported that the best adjustments to retirement occurred when the retirees worked in jobs or fields related to their main careers or where the retirees have considerable knowledge. The researchers determined that health improvements did not accrue to those retirees trying to adapt to new job conditions and different work environments, which caused greater stress.

Improving your health conditions through continuing to work in retirement seems to be true in other developed countries also. A 14 year study, conducted by Hadassah Hospital Mount Scopus in Jerusalem, obtained significant results. The 1000 participants were all aged 70 when they entered the study. The researchers determined that persons still working at this age were 2.5 times more likely to be alive at age 82 than those who had retired and were not working at age 70.

Here is a possible situation which could apply to many of us. As you review your retirement budget, you realize another $15,000 per year or $1250 per month would make your lifestyle much more enjoyable. A goal might be your wish to trade in your SUV gas guzzler for a new $25,000 hybrid, but without added income, you would have to go in debt or liquidate savings. The extra $15,000 income would do the trick. In addition, the part time work could help you achieve other goals, such as your $13,000 dream river cruise down the Danube. These are just a few examples of special things made possible by still working some after retirement.

How do you locate a part time job which will pay you the $12,000 to $18,000 per year you desire? Minimum wage jobs will <u>not</u> generate the $1000 to $1500 per month you wish without working nearly full time. If you are willing to work full time, remaining on your original job may be the best decision. I can't emphasize enough, **"Don't jump into retirement without thoroughly researching your options."** Costly mistakes may occur when you cut your ties before you know the results.

Depending upon your skills, many options are open to you. You may be able to consult with your old firm, but many times you cannot continue your pension while you work for them. In 2006 the Pension Protection Act began allowing firms to alter their pension plans to provide for partial distributions to employees under a phased retirement program. Not every firm has qualified their pension plans, so check with your Human Relations or Personnel Department to see if this is an option for you.

Another way to receive a pension, while you work for your previous company, is to be represented by a professional placement firm. This organization normally provides candidates to fill temporary positions. This way you can receive your pension while you consult or work with your old firm. There may be a placement fee, but many times this is paid by the firm who temporarily employs you. Generally, you will not receive benefits for the temporary job, but many times you will receive a higher income, allowing you to pay for your own benefits. You may also be performing the role of an independent contractor, allowing self-employment tax benefits.

Your special skills and knowledge may allow you to consult with other firms. Also, there are temporary agencies who specialize in filling short term professional and executive positions. These positions may only be needed for three to six months, while the firm searches for a replacement to fill a key job. The risk is, if the firm likes your handling of the job, you will become a candidate for full time employment.

Ways of creating income after retirement are as numerous as your imagination will provide. Expanding your hobby into a paying business is always a possibility. One example is a amateur wood worker who filled a need occurring as people downsized their homes. This created the desire for multi-purpose rooms, such as the spare bedroom, used both as an office and a guest bedroom. The increasing popularity of the wall mounted, Murphy bed, gave him his new opportunity. Providing custom service to his friends and relatives got him started. He could control his income and the amount he worked by the number of units he sold. By providing a special service, promoted mostly by word of mouth, it allowed him to clear nearly $15,000 per year, working only part time. His only problem was, he became so popular he kept being pushed toward a full time business.

Many hobbies of the ladies of the household have great part time business potential. The renewed popularity of quilting has provided excellent supplemental income opportunities. Owning a long arm quilting machine, designed for high speed quilting, permits the owner to complete other's partially done quilts. Most quilters love to put together the decorative quilt top and the backing, but they hate the tedious, time consuming assembly and hand quilting process. For a fee, the long arm quilting machine owner assembles the quilt and quilts the pattern desired by the quilt owner. The assembly and quilting is achieved in a tenth of the time it requires to complete by hand.

The quilting machine owners many times will create their own quilts or decorative wall hangings, which can be readily sold at fairs and craft shows. This is an excellent example of a low cost business, operated from your home. The main expense is the $15,000 cost of a good long arm quilting machine. Many of the hobby type home businesses can be operated in residential areas, with minimal commercial permit requirements. Your income is mainly dictated by how much time you are willing to devote to your business.

Another ideal home business is authorship. Many of you have wanted to write and publish books, but lacked the time and knowledge. Early retirement can finally provide you the opportunity. If this will be your first publication, I recommend working with an author's coach, such as Ann McIndoo, my coach. The correct approach to authorship will make your efforts efficient and effective, while attempting it on your own may lead you to some real challenges. Ms. McIndoo will help you publish a truly marketable book in one tenth of the time of your doing it entirely on your own. A good start would be to contact Ann at www.SoYouWantToWrite.com for excellent ideas on how to begin your new career as an author.

The food service industry has many good opportunities for part time employment. A high end restaurant and/or bar has a cyclical pattern to their staffing requirements. An example In the Northwest is a quality seafood restaurant chain, which uses many wait and bar staff only on Friday, Saturday and Sunday. With a good wage, plus tips, the staff averages about $150 per day, or nearly $2000, working only 13 days per month. In addition, anyone working 24 hours or more per week qualifies for health care benefits.

The East Coast of the U.S. has a unique need for food service or tourism help for only about six months of the year. In the Northeast, New Hampshire, Vermont and Maine operate many of their restaurant and hospitality businesses seasonally. They close in early October, reopening in April of the following year. Many of the businesses and staff move to Florida for the winter to continue working or to enjoy the sun. The reverse occurs in Florida, when the tourism activities slow in the spring, and the businesses and staff move back north to either continue their operations or enjoy six months of leisure. Similar patterns occur in the Southwest Deserts, trading back and forth between the Pacific Northwest or Canada, as the seasons dictate.

Other seasonal employment opportunities for persons retiring from sales or marketing careers, or who are comfortable meeting the public, can earn an excellent income working the summer fair circuit. You may sell or demonstrate products from booths at the various fairs. Or, you can purchase a portable food service van or trailer, which can be moved from fair to fair. You will work extremely hard for four months or so, but then you can head for Arizona or Florida to join the snowbird set. The Internet again is a excellent resource for information regarding the fair circuit businesses. Try contacting the headquarters for the major fairs in your area and they can provide you with a wealth of information regarding job opportunities. Display spaces and vendors must be approved by the fair board or staff, so start making contacts early, preferably a year in advance of any potential fair circuit.

If you have joined the deluxe gypsies of the RV lifestyle, gatherings of RV'ers in areas such as Quartzsite, Arizona, near Highway 10 in Western Arizona, provide numerous income opportunities. In January

4-Star Retirement 2-Star Budget

and February of each year, 2000 vendors of rocks, gems, minerals and fossils, plus everything else you can find at major flea markets, gather to sell their wares. This community, of less than 2000 population, attracts over one million visitors each year, including snowbirds, collectors and enthusiasts. Over 500,000 RV'ers are scattered over many square miles of the Bureau of Land Management desert lands surrounding Quartzsite. If you have handcrafts to sell or services to provide, the annual madhouse is the place to be. Many vendors pay for the rest of their winter escape from their Quartzsite excursion.

Another part time money making opportunity, particularly for the RV owner or someone living close to one of Amazon's 34 North American distribution centers, is to work the end-of-year rush. Nearly 40 percent of Amazon's sales occur in the fourth quarter, with numerous part time workers needed to handle the added volume. Many of their distribution centers quadruple their employment during this period. Qualified seniors are welcome, and the approximately $12 per hour makes it possible to earn $4000 to $5000 in the period before year's end. For a snowbird RV'er this can cover most of their costs of snowbirding. Others, living close to distribution centers, have the same opportunity to supplement their income. Walmart, Target and other large retail distribution centers have similar programs.

Many retired individuals work part time at Big Box Stores such as Costco. The demonstrators of food and other products typically earn $11 per hour, during a 6 hour shift, which is well above minimum wage. They also need part time people for restocking, boxing at checkout, plus entrance or exit greeters. Most work 12 to 24 hours per week, with matching 401k benefits after one year. If you are physically able to stand for six hours, any age may be employed. Most of their hiring is done through a firm known as Warehouse Demos Provider, www.wdsdemos.com.

Anyone retiring before age 65, prior to qualifying for Medicare, must plan for a possible major healthcare expense. While working full time, much of this expense has been born by your previous employer. Many large employers extend your healthcare coverage into retirement, until you are eligible for Medicare, but numerous smaller companies do not have this benefit. You are then faced with this major expense, or you need to find a job which will pick up all or a portion of these costs. As Sam and Martha learned, typical health care premiums for a couple are at least $1200 to $1500 per month.

A definite consideration is to **locate an employer who will provide health care benefits to part time employees.** Usually, it will require working at least 20 hours per week to qualify for the benefit program. You may find benefits playing a bigger role than hourly earnings when looking for a part time job in retirement. When interviewing for a new job, don't be afraid to discuss healthcare benefits.

After age 50 most people have some pre-existing health conditions, such as high blood pressure or diabetes, which may allow insurance companies to deny coverage, or exclude coverage for the existing conditions. If your healthcare benefits will stop when taking early retirement, begin looking for alternate coverage at least 60 days before you are dropped from your old program. It may easily require 30 to 60 days to find new coverage.

Something worth considering is the COBRA program, which requires your old company to retain you under their group plan for 18 months after you leave, as long as you pay 100% of your premiums. The COBRA program, (Consolidated Omnibus Budget Reconciliation Act of 1985) guarantees continuing group health coverage for employees working at companies with 20 or more people. The 18 months of coverage may allow you to convert to an individual plan without restrictions for your pre-existing conditions. You may also wish to look into group insurance available through your Professional or Social Associations.

Part time work during the early part of your retirement may allow you to delay receiving Social Security benefits until you reach your full benefit age. For today's Boomers, full Social Security will occur at age 66 or 67. Delaying Social Security until age 70, will provide an even greater retirement premium, especially if you anticipate living into your mid-90's. Starting Social Security at age 62 will reduce your benefits by 25%, compared with your normal retirement age. Each year you delay starting Social Security your monthly benefits gain approximately 8%, which is better than most of our other investments.

Keep part time work as a viable option, when taking early retirement. Working part time after retiring is a great insurance plan in its own right. Not only do you add to your income, but it gives you an easier entry back into full time employment, if something occurs to upset your lifestyle. It also keeps your brain working and makes life more stimulating.

NORMAL RETIREMENT AGE

Many of you use the age when full Social Security benefits are paid as normal retirement age. Others look for age 65, when they qualify for Medicare. Although Medicare qualification begins at age 65, Social Security uses a variable scale, based upon your income, time worked and date of birth. The early boomers, born between 1943 and 1954, reach full Social Security benefits at age 66. Those born in 1955 reach full benefits at age 66, plus 2 months, while those born in 1959, qualify at age 66, plus 10 months. In 2012, full benefits don't begin until you reach age 67.

You may wish to begin your Social Security benefits as early as age 62, receiving an amount 25% less than if you waited until your full benefit age. You will still receive the same amount of benefits over your estimated average lifetime, which is 83 for a man at age 65 and 85 for a woman at age 65. Even if you start Social Security benefits at age 62, receiving a 25% reduction, you will receive more months of benefits. This is based upon the assumption of your living to age 83, and you receiving benefits for 21 years, when started at age 62. By waiting until age 66, you may only receive the higher benefits for 17 years, but your larger monthly checks will equal the lesser amount paid over the 21 years.

Another consideration is to delay your Social Security until age 70. For each year you delay, your benefits will increase approximately 8%, until age 70. Using the average age expectancy tables, you will still receive the same total amount, as if your checks began at your standard full Social Security age. But, if you expect to be one of the 25% who live to be 90 or one of the 10% to exceed age 95, the added benefits can be significant.

If you continue to work after beginning early Social Security benefits, your benefits will be reduced by $1 for every $2 you earn, above the 2012 limit of $14,640. The deductions may vary each year, so check with Social Security for your particular situation. In their attempt to be fair, the Social Security Administration keeps track of any reductions in your benefit checks prior to your full benefit age. At the time of your full benefit age, your monthly checks will be increased enough to repay any prior benefit reductions.

Thoroughly investigate your Social Security options long before you make the jump to retirement living. Social Security benefits vary greatly depending upon your income over your working life and your age. Please check with the Social Security Administration for a more exacting benefit amount and qualification. A good resource is online at www.ssa.gov. You will find Benefit Calculators, Age Tables and other important information, but it may be better to check with a Social Security agent for exact amounts.

Chapter Eight

Taxes Matter in Retirement

Overall, the structure of your State and Local tax system may have a greater impact on your financial health than you think. Here are just a few of the taxes you may be faced with, over and above all of your Federal taxes:

☆ Personal State and Local Income Tax
☆ Business Income Tax
☆ State, County and Local Sales Tax
☆ Property Tax
☆ Business and Occupational Gross Tax
☆ Gasoline, Cigarette and Alcohol Tax
☆ Miscellaneous Fees and Permits
☆ Estate Taxes

The Tax Foundation, located in Washington, D.C., as well as the Federation of Tax Administrators, analyze National, State and Local tax matters, as statistics become available. Their nationwide, on-line data may help you visualize living in other cities and states. Finding lower tax rates and fees can help stretch your retirement dollars.

When you average all of the various state and local taxes residents pay, New Jersey, New York and Connecticut stand head and shoulders above the rest. Their state and local taxes equal 12.0 to 12.2 percent of a resident's income. The rest of the top 10 highest state and local tax states are: Wisconsin, Rhode Island, California, Minnesota, Vermont, Maine and Pennsylvania. They range from 11.0 down to 10.1 percent state and local taxes.

Here is a comparison between the highest States and the lowest for total average State and Local Taxes:

Combined State and Local Taxes			
Highest %		Lowest %	
New Jersey	12.2	Alaska	6.3
New York	12.1	Nevada	7.5
Connecticut	12.0	South Dakota	7.6
Wisconsin	11.0	Tennessee	7.6
Rhode Island	10.7	Wyoming	7.8
California	10.6	Texas	7.9
Minnesota	10.3	New Hampshire	8.0
Vermont	10.2	South Carolina	8.1
Maine	10.1	Louisiana	8.2
Pennsylvania	10.1	New Mexico	8.4

The total State and Local tax percentages will not impact each of you in the same way. Your annual retirement income and its source, plus your style of living will definitely affect your spendable income. Such things as holdings of high valued real estate, in a high Property Tax state or municipality, may have a greater impact than State Income Tax on your retirement cash flow. State and Local Sales Taxes are the next variable as you look for the ideal location to retire.

Many times, states with tax rates low in one category, such as Income Tax, make up the difference with high Sales or Property Taxes. Don't let the fun you had on a special vacation be the main factor when determining where to retire. Take a hard look at State and Local Taxes before making your final decision. Here are some recent State Income Tax rates, comparing the high and low:

State Income Tax Rates

Highest %		Lowest %	
Hawaii	11.0	Alaska, Florida, Nevada,	
Oregon	11.0	S. Dakota, Texas, Wash., &	
California	10.6	Wyoming – All	0.0
Rhode Island	9.9	Arizona	4.54
Vermont	9.4	Alabama, N.H.	5.0
Iowa, N.J., N.Y.	9.0	Mississippi	5.0

The tax rates for residential property, occupied by the owner, vary greatly throughout the United States. The States may have laws governing the annual tax rate or the maximum which can be collected for a given category, but each county within a state may have different property tax rates. The formulas for setting taxable real estate values, as well as the ultimate annual tax collected, generally vary from about 0.3% to 3.0% of your property's market value. A good method for researching real estate property tax rates is to web search the Department of Revenue within any state you are considering. Other tax rate sources include the Assessor's office in a given county or from the Realtor you are dealing with.

Sales or use tax rates vary by state, county and municipality, similar to real estate property taxes. The states tend to set a base sales tax rate, and then the counties and municipalities add one to three percentage points to the state rates for their own particular needs. Some of the basic state sales tax rate percentages are:

Basic Sales Tax Rates			
California	7.25	Alaska	0.0
Indiana	7.00	Delaware	0.0
New Jersey	7.00	Montana	0.0
Rhode Island	7.00	N. Hampshire	0.0
Tennessee	7.00	Oregon	0.0

An important consideration of where to live during retirement is the major variation in how your retirement income is taxed within the different states. The National Conference of State Legislatures, www.ncsl.org, has an excellent study, published in 2011, entitled, "STATE PERSONAL INCOME TAXES ON RETIREMENT INCOME: TAX YEAR 2010." They found, of the states levying a personal income tax, most allow people to exclude at least a part of their retirement income from state income tax. There were five states which **did not** exclude any retirement income from state income tax. These states are California, Nebraska, North Dakota, Rhode Island and Vermont.

As mentioned earlier, Alaska, Florida, Nevada, South Dakota, Texas Washington and Wyoming do not have an income tax, while New Hampshire and Tennessee personal income tax applies only on dividend and interest income. Of the remaining 41 states with a personal income tax, 36 provide exclusions for some or all of the following retirement income:

- ☆ Local, State or Federal Pensions
- ☆ Federal Civil Service Pension
- ☆ Military Pension
- ☆ Social Security
- ☆ Private Pension

Although the policies for taxation on retirement income vary greatly between the different states, they do tend to have two things in common. The states wish to protect the incomes of taxpayers no longer in the workforce, and/or they use the retirement income tax exclusion to attract retired people or retain retirees within the state.

An exercise during the first year after retirement is to visualize your retirement lifestyle, were you to live in a different state or municipality. Wait until you have adjusted to your new cash flow, as well as your style of living. This could be a good time to hit the library or go online to research the financial aspects of moving. Document projections of your cost of living in desired states and communities. If you live in California, then look at nearby Nevada. Nevada has no income tax and low housing costs, while California's income tax can be around 10% or more and no retirement income exclusions.

Always at least compare the following:

- ☆ Income Taxes
- ☆ Sales Tax
- ☆ Real Estate Tax
- ☆ Estate Tax

Federal taxes and how you handle them can also have a large impact on the success of your long term retirement. Efficient income tax handling by retirees is a very individualized matter, and the following information should not be the sole basis for your financial decisions. It is not intended as advice to meet the needs of an individual investor. Always keep your investment advisor or tax advisor in the loop when making major investment and tax decisions.

Almost every retiree will be faced with how best to liquidate retirement assets. Research by professor William Reichenstein, of Baylor University determined, if you simply sequence your withdrawals from your investments, your savings nest egg may last two to five years longer. As discussed in my **Chapter Four: Are Your Finances Ready?**, to make your nest egg last the necessary 25 to 30 retirement years, plan to withdraw no more than 3 to 5% of your nest egg annually. Rather than withdrawing the classic 4% plus inflation, withdrawing 3 to 5% of your total nest egg annually will automatically adjust to inflation. Cut back in a down year, and save the excess in a good year. Reichenstein's general rules of thumb for sequencing the withdrawal of funds from your investment accounts are:

☆ Tap your taxable accounts first.
☆ Next withdraw from tax deferred IRA's and 401k's.
☆ Lastly, spend from the tax free ROTH IRA'S.

Research your tax consequences before you make any changes to your tax deferred savings. The U.S. Tax Code has many mine fields requiring caution on your part when making major monetary decisions. Penalties such as the 10% deduction when with-drawing funds from your tax deferred savings accounts prior to age 59 1/2. This is in addition to paying full income tax on the amount withdrawn due to its addition to your adjusted gross income. There are a number of exceptions to the penalty, such as certain hurricane repairs, down payments for a primary residence, rolling over into another approved, tax deferred account within 60 days and a loan paid back within 5 years, etc. Many of these types of tax laws change annually, at the whims of our politicians and regulators. Do your homework before you change.

When you reach age 70 1/2 tax laws require a Required Minimum Distribution from your tax deferred accounts, such as your IRA's. Any ROTH IRA's are excluded from the RMD, which is another reason your ROTH's can be such an important element of your retirement savings. Based upon the IRS Uniform Lifetime Table, the year you reach age 70 1/2, you must remove approximately 3.65% of the total in your regular IRA , based upon December 31 of the year prior to your birthday. The distribution increases each year, with about 6.76% required distribution from the IRA total as of December 31 prior to your 85th birthday. Were you to live to 115 years old, you would still distribute 52.6% of your regular IRA balance. Please remember, all liquidations from your deferred tax accounts, will be added to your gross income and will be taxed as regular income.

The Required Minimum Distribution from your regular IRA at age 70 1/2 is a good example of why your financial planning in retirement is not a "Set it and forget it" proposition. Plan ahead for known events, such as the RMD, when you will have new taxable income, whether you want it or not. This again is where your personal financial or tax advisor can be of great help. The RMD is a type of sequencing over which you have little or no control. Look for reallocation of your investments or assets, to keep from being pushed unnecessarily into a higher tax bracket.

Those of you wishing to operate your own full or part time business in retirement, as we discussed in **Chapter Seven**, need to consider taxation and business climate. Here again, your financial advisor can help. He or she can recommend the best business structure, whether Sole Proprietor, Limited Liability Company or Schedule S Corporation. A legitimate small business has many tax advantages, such as expensing business travel, computer equipment, office space and furniture, related memberships and publications, etc. Plus, it's nice to supplement your income while doing something you like.

Before taking the plunge into a new business, possibly in a new location, you need to study the business tax structure in your State compared to others. In a 2012 study, by the Tax Foundation, ranking all 50 states for their Business Climate, the State and Local Taxes were major factors in the ratings. Top and bottom 10 were:

Business Tax Structure	
Best States	**Worst States**
1 Wyoming	41 Iowa
2 South Dakota	42 Maryland
3 Nevada	43 Wisconsin
4 Alaska	44 North Carolina
5 Florida	45 Minnesota
6 New Hampshire	46 Rhode Island
7 Washington	47 Vermont
8 Montana	48 California
9 Texas	49 New York
10 Utah	50 New Jersey

Operating a business close to the border of a State which has tax rates complementary to your business is worth considering. A firm located in Vancouver, WA, without an income tax, across the border from Portland, OR, which doesn't have a sales tax, can enhance your profits.

The most important thing to remember is, time and effort devoted to learning of tax variations in different locations can be a great investment toward a long and prosperous retirement. The Tax Code, if used wisely, can be a great assist to your financial health. If you have a financial or tax advisor, especially one with a working knowledge of your finances and goals, they will likely be your best research resource. Financial advisors on line, such as Retiree Inc. and ESPlanner are noted as reputable firms, but it's always a risk providing private information to someone you don't know well. For a fee of $150 to $1000, ESP or Retiree Inc. will develop plans designed to give you the best standard of living or the most efficient use of your retirement funds.

Chapter Nine

Making Every Dollar Count

You have worked long and hard to earn your successful retirement, let's look at some ways to ensure your lifestyle will remain comfortable over the next 25 or 30 years. Much of your spending patterns in retirement will depend on your mindset. Whether you are more concerned about keeping up with your neighbors or your brother-in-law, versus getting the best value for every dollar you spend, may determine how long your retirement funds will last.

During the 35 to 45 years of your working career, you may have found, like many of us, things had become very important in your life. Things such as, living in the nicest house in the neighborhood, driving the newest car, belonging to the golf and country club or eating out two or three times per week, played key roles in your everyday life. As you retire, or get ready to retire, review just how significant these "feel good" items will be as you allocate your available retirement funds over the next 25 or 30 years.

Ideally, before you retire, or soon after retirement, you should analyze your household budget. It may be of interest to compare your expenditures with those of a typical couple, aged 58, with a household annual, before tax income of $75,312 and after tax income of $72,457. The Bureau of Labor Statistics found 27,000,000 households in this category with allocations of:

☆ Housing	31.39%
☆ Transportation	17.54%
☆ Personal Insurance, Pensions & Savings	11.69%
☆ Food	11.64%
☆ Healthcare	8.12%
☆ Entertainment	6.23%
☆ Cash Contributions	4.43%
☆ Apparel and Services	2.92%
☆ Miscellaneous	1.64%
☆ Education	1.44%
☆ Personal Care Products & Services	1.22%
☆ Alcoholic Beverages	0.95%
☆ Tobacco Products & Smoking Supplies	0.52%
☆ Reading	0.29%
☆ Total	100.0%

The next step in the retirement spending process is to look for the most realistic categories to cut back or downsize, in order to adjust to your anticipated retirement income. A simple way to start is to list your own monthly expenses, as listed in the Bureau of Labor Statics study of 2008. Then, assuming you need to reduce expenses approximately $1,000 per month or about 16% of your pre-retirement income, to make everything work out, decide where to cut. Look first to your major categories, where the biggest dollars are found. Then start by deducting the same 16 percent from each category, and finally, adjust your expenditures between the various categories until you feel you have a livable lifestyle:

4-Star Retirement 2-Star Budget

Reduced Budget		
Category	**Current**	**Final Budget**
Housing	$2000	$1500
Transportation	$1100	$ 915
Food	$ 730	$ 610
Entertainment	$ 390	$ 290
Cash Contributions	$ 280	$ 185

In order to reduce your housing costs by $500 per month some major changes are called for. Your home of over 15 years has a balance owing of $150,000, and it should sell fairly quickly at $340,000. After 10% selling costs and payment of the underlying mortgage you will net $155,000. A nice 2 bedroom, 2 bath, 1600 square foot condo is available for $200,000. You can pay $150,000 down, leaving an easy 5 year mortgage at $920 per month, including interest at 4% per annum. After $2000 annual property tax, $3600 home owner's association fees and estimated $1200 maintenance and miscellaneous costs, you are within your $1500 per month budget. Plus, you will own a beautiful condo without the headaches of outside maintenance, and it will be free and clear within 5 years. Once the condo is paid off, which fits the philosophy of not carrying mortgage debt very far into retirement, you will have an additional $11,000 per year to spend.

To trim $185 per month from your car expense you have several options. You can sell the least used car, and buy a slightly older vehicle, eliminating or reducing your payments. You can reduce insurance costs by upping the collision deductible to $500 or even $1000. You can save $80 per month by washing the car yourself, rather than paying $20 per week at the local car wash. After retirement, there is even a chance you can get by nicely with only one car, especially if you buy a condo in a good shopping and public transportation location.

Lowering your food and entertainment costs are as simple as eating out only twice per month and on special occasions, rather than weekly. Also, the more time available after retirement will allow shopping the grocery ads and utilizing coupons to get the best values. The come-on ads and coupons are just to get you in the store, where they expect you to do your entire shopping. By only purchasing the special sale products, which many times are loss leaders, your extra shopping time will be well compensated by your substantial savings. In retirement you will not be faced with as many office fund raisers or donation requests, easily saving another $100 per month.

To keep from tapping into your retirement nest egg unnecessarily, you might consider some other major changes. You belong to the golf and country club, with dues of $300 per month, plus a food and beverage purchase requirement of $125 per month. An alternative is a nice local public golf course, with an age 55 and older men's club for $100 per year and play any weekday for $25, including cart. This may lack some of the prestige of a country club, but you keep your handicap established, maintain fellowship, while saving $3500 per year.

After your home, your cars take the next biggest chunk from your monthly budget. Nothing can duplicate the feeling and smell of your first drive home in a brand new car. The ooh's and aah's from your friends and neighbors can't help but boost your pride, but it comes at a price. Your car typically loses 25% of its value the day you sign the papers and drive it off the dealer's lot. Buying the same model 10 months later, with 10,000 miles on the odometer, and another 25,000 miles of new car warranty, will save you $10,000. You will get many more points by using the $10,000 savings to take your spouse on an anniversary cruise to Tahiti, rather than the feelings of driving a new car home. In addition, keep the car in good condition for another 5 to 7 years, and it will be worth about the same as the $40,000, brand new car you passed up.

When you look at the person in the bathroom mirror each morning, you see the one most responsible for the success of your retirement finances. When you were committed to at least 60 hours per week of work and commute time, you didn't always have time to try to save money. You ate out two or three times per week, because both you and your partner were too tired to cook. You used a commercial car wash each week, a yard maintenance service mowed your lawn and weeded your flower beds and you hired contractors to paint walls or repair plumbing. These items easily add up to $1,000's each year. You now have the time to do these items yourself and pocket the $1,000's of savings.

Discipline and patience rate high on the list of needs for sound money management in retirement. Instant gratification has become a way of life for many of us. If you want something, you may buy it now, even without the needed cash. Instead you just hand over your credit card, planning to pay it off at the end of the month. But when the bill comes due your car needs a new set of tires for $700, which you add to your credit card. Now your total credit card bill is $1000, and you are a little short of cash. The credit card company will gladly accept a minimum $50 payment on your $1000 bill. The next month the total bill is $1500, but again you are a little short of cash, so you pay $100, planning to catch up later.

Once you get on this slippery slope of credit card debt, it is hard to get off. This is how people of modest means end up owing $20,000 or more, in credit card debt, at 11 to 16% interest. The card companies love it, for $20,000 of debt at 14% costs over $230 per month in interest. The interest on $20,000 or so of credit card debt may cost you nearly $3000 per year. When you are working full time, with a few years until retirement, make every effort to reduce your debts. Once you are faced with fixed income in retirement, out of control debt can lead to poverty.

A workable solution, before you get into serious debt trouble, establish a Cash Management Account with the firm handling your investments.

Your total credit card charges will be settled at the same time each month by deducting from your cash account. This will eliminate your building a high interest debt balance, but there is still the danger of liquidating too much of your savings. Once again, consistently review your financial and nest egg balances. Study your budget, or establish a workable budget, to be certain your assets will last as long as you do.

If you haven't done so, establish or re-establish realistic financial goals. Build a cash or highly liquid six month reserve to cover your expenses, in case an emergency or unexpected expenses occur. A medical emergency, a market crash or a car accident are never planned, but they do happen, and you may be faced with a major drain from your savings. Another type of goal is replacement of an expensive asset such as your car. Your car will be seven years old in four years, and a replacement will cost around $35,000. In a little over 5 years, depositing $500 per month in an account earning 4% per annum will provide you the $35,000 for your new car. Just keep the dollars in an account that's not easy to tap if you all of a sudden need a few bucks.

Many thrifty living suggestions include shopping with coupons, buying at yard sales and thrift stores and other small types of savings. This can become almost a full time job. Instead, find your savings from your big four categories of housing, transportation, food and entertainment, which total 2/3's of your typical budget. Make meaningful budget savings without taking away all the fun of retirement.

Chapter Ten

Healthy Retirement

    This chapter will explore your health risks, along with their potential impacts, and how you can manage them to achieve your best possible retirement. Our personal health is something many of us don't think a lot about. If we get sick, we see the doctor and get it fixed. Since the end of World War II, even though we have tended to neglect our health, the improving medical technologies and reduced smoking, have kept us living healthier and longer lives. But, now our neglect is catching up with us, and the number of seniors developing disabling health problems is beginning to increase.

    The rising cost and discomfort of disabilities may be your greatest risk that could keep you from living a productive, affordable and enjoyable retirement. In general, our health is slipping, with about two-thirds of Medicaid spending and more than one-third of Medicare costs needed to handle our disabilities. This may lead to our pocket books taking a major hit, for these entitlements only cover a portion of our disability costs. Journals of Gerontology reported in December of 2012, that between 2000 and 2005 (the latest data available), persons older than 65, needing help with areas of daily living, such as dressing, feeding themselves and mobility, increased 9 percent. The American Journal of Public Health reported in January of 2012, individuals 60 and over had significant increases in almost all kinds of disabilities, when comparing the periods 1988-1994 to the 1999-2004 time frame.

The trends we are experiencing in the health and disabilities of those in retirement or approaching retirement are scary. Teresa Seeman, professor of medicine and epidemiology at UCLA and co-author of the American Journal of Public Health article, found disability rates increasing most for 60 to 69 year-olds. These were individuals born during and just after WWII, entering adulthood in the 1960's, when obesity was increasing as a health risk. The Boomers, our next generation, accelerated this weight gain tendency. Now, weight gain has become a major contributor to the higher incidence of disabilities occurring.

Approximately 2 out of every 3 individuals in the U.S.A. are overweight or obese, with one study estimating 60 million or 30% of the adult population obese. In another study, in the period 2007-2008, the National Health and Nutrition Examination Survey estimated the adult population to be 68 percent overweight or obese. They consider obesity a disease affecting 34 percent of adults age 20 and over. The study found 32.2 percent of men and 35.5 of women in American to be obese.

A measure known as the Body Mass Index is used to determine if you have normal weight for your height, or if you fall above or below normal. The following formula will allow you to calculate your own BMI:

Measuring Using Inches and Pounds:
- ☆ (Weight in pounds) divided by (height in inches squared)
- ☆ Times the number 703 equals BMI. For example, if your weight is 175 lbs. and height 65 in. (175 divided by 65 squared) X 703 = BMI of 29.1

Measuring Using kilograms and Meters:
- ☆ (Kilograms of weight) div. by (meters of height squared)
- ☆ 79.4 div. by 2.73 = BMI of 29.1

The generally accepted standards for BMI results are:

BMI	Weight Status
Below 18.5	Underweight
18.5 - 24.9	Normal
25.0 - 29.9	Overweight
30.0 and above	Obese

On-line calculators, where you just enter your height and weight, are available. Check with your doctor to see if your BMI indicates a weight problem requiring action.

Dr. Mehmet Oz, a cardiothoracic surgeon, who many view on ABC's Doctor Oz Show, has an easy measurement to determine if you are overweight. Your waist measurement should be equal or less than one half of your height. A man, 5 foot 10 inches, or 70 inches, should not go over a 35 inch waist. A five foot four inch woman should not exceed a 32 inch waist. A 35 inch waist for women and a 40 inch waist for men is the upper limit before being considered obese. Your doctor is your best source to review a combination of your BMI, waist size and height to help determine if your weight is acceptable or if something needs to be done about it. Well-developed muscles weigh more than fat, so an athlete may carry more weight for their height than an average person. Due to the great variability between individuals, a professional, should help make the final determination of your own acceptable weight range.

Weight gain is another slippery slope item. It usually has occurred over many years, allowing you to adjust to and accept (rationalize) the gradual increase in your body mass and shape. The irony is, although the developed world has been facing major risks from an overweight population for years, the media is just beginning to publicize the health dangers we face. Unless our media considers something a crisis or a catastrophe, they don't give it much print space or air time. They seem engrossed in waving red flags about climate change and pushing alternative energy, neither of which pose the level of threats to our lives as does obesity, The media has continually ignored the overweight population issue. It's like smoking, where they accept over 400,000 related deaths per year as normal, and do little to reduce smoking impacts. The media and our politicians have accepted the millions who die each year from diseases related to the overweight crisis and unhealthy lifestyles, as a normal outgrowth of the developed world. **A sad position.**

It is predicted that 1/5th or 21% of our 2018 medical costs will be related to obesity. Nancy Hellmich, *USA Today,* reported in 2009 that a study by America's Health Rankings, found the United States was spending about $1.8 trillion per year on medical costs associated with chronic diseases. These include diabetes, heart disease, stroke and cancer, and all four were linked in some degree to smoking and/or obesity. They found nearly 1 in 5 adults still smoke, leading to over 400,000 related deaths per year. Obesity is the next greatest link to chronic diseases and death. Ms. Hellmich documented studies estimating health care costs, associated with just obesity, reaching $344,000 billion annually by 2018.

The U.S. Department of Health and Human Services, through their National Center for Health Statistics, found at age 60 and over, we average nearly 40% obesity. Women were 42.3% obese, up from the 36.0% for women in the 40-59 age group. Men have leveled out at 36.6% in the 60 and over category, down from 37.2% in the 40-59 age group. Anyone in the obese category exposes themselves to dangerous consequences. Obesity increases your risk of developing high blood pressure, type 2 diabetes, heart disease, stroke, gallbladder disease, age-related macular degeneration (AMD) and cancers of the breast, prostate and colon. And, **the greatest risk of all, your risk of death.**

Below is the geographic obesity pattern in the U.S.:

Most Obese	**Least Obese**
1. Mississippi	51. Colorado
2. Alabama	50. Wash., D.C.
3. West Virginia	49. Connecticut
4. Tennessee	48. Massachusetts
5. Louisiana	47. Hawaii
6. Kentucky	46. Utah
7. Oklahoma	45. Vermont
8. South Carolina	44. Montana
9. Arkansas	43. New Jersey
10. Michigan	42. Rhode Island

Preliminary results of 2010 death rates per 100,000 population, by state, from the National Vital Statistics Reports correlate the death risks to rates of obesity. The study found that the 9 states with the highest death rates were also the 9 states with the highest obesity rates. Their accumulation of data from each state found the following death rate ranking per 100,000 population:

Highest Death Rates	**Lowest Death Rates**
1. Mississippi	51. Hawaii
2. Alabama	50. California
3. West Virginia	49. Connecticut
4. Oklahoma	48. Minnesota
5. Kentucky	47. New York
6. Louisiana	46. Massachusetts
7. Arkansas	45. Colorado
8. Tennessee	44. New Hampshire
9. South Carolina	43. New Jersey
10. Georgia	42. Washington

Chapter Ten

What has caused this major epidemic of obesity and overweight, and what can we do about it?

A lot of the problem is caused by major lifestyle changes occurring after World War II. Prior to WWII you had much more physical labor burning your calories. Many of you worked on farms or were employed in factories producing goods without the modern automation used today. You mowed the lawn with a push mower, raised much of your food in a home garden, cut wood without a chainsaw, hung clothes to dry on a line in the backyard, cleaned carpets with a manual carpet sweeper, you stood as you washed dishes by hand, after preparing meals without a microwave, etc. Your prewar lifestyle had a great deal more manual labor than you do today, but **you are still eating the same number or more calories than you did years ago.**

Today, much of your work is done with a keyboard, Ipad, power tools, dishwasher or microwave. Urban lifestyle, with an apartment, condo or a minimum care landscaped home, requiring little physical labor, is the norm. Both partners working, coming home tired and rushed, encourages our eating out, or depending on fast food and/or convenience foods. Obtaining a large percentage of your calories from these sources may lead you into the overweight/obese population, so prevalent in the current developed world.

You work so hard for 30, 40 or 50 years toward a long and enjoyable retirement, but then, if you don't care for your health, it all goes for naught. The sad thing, according to data from the National Vital Statistics Reports, is the top six diseases in the U.S., including heart disease, cancer, lung disease, stroke, Alzheimer's, and diabetes, account for the deaths of 1.6 million Americans each year. This annual death toll almost equals the total military deaths in U.S. history, from the Revolutionary War to the war in Afghanistan. A major portion of these deaths relate to smoking, obesity and a sedentary lifestyle, most of which you can control. Diabetes alone accounts for twice as many deaths annually, as does the automobile, yet the evening news never reports deaths from diabetes. The long-term complications from high blood sugar and diabetes can lead to heart disease, strokes, blindness, kidney failure and limb amputation, due to poor circulation, and finally, your life may be shortened by up to 10 years from the effects of diabetes. These facts scare me, and I hope they get your attention also.

Only you can motivate yourself to live the healthy lifestyle. Let's explore ways you can control your weight problem, if you are one of the two out of three overweight or obese persons in the U.S. None of us intentionally harm our health, but many of the highest health risks don't hurt, ache or bleed. This allows you to ignore these risks until they develop into a serious disease. You may plan to join the gym the first of next month, or to begin a new diet on Monday, after the office picnic. Somehow, it doesn't happen, with other things seeming to take precedence over controlling your weight and long term health.

There are only three things which will bring you to or keep you within the acceptable range of your Body Mass Index or B.M.I.:
1. Your **exercise**
2. Your **diet**
3. Your **attitude**

Your willingness to eat a proper diet and exercise regularly are the keys to maintaining your health in retirement. But, like most worthwhile things in life, it will take work and effort on your part to achieve your weight and fitness goals. If the risks of shortening your life by 10 years, limb amputation, loss of eye sight or requiring a wheel chair or a cane doesn't get your attention, nothing will

Proper diet will be covered later, but first, let's look at the exercise and fitness side of the equation. The Group Health Cooperative, of Washington State, is a leader in Preventative Medicine. They describe fitness as "Being able to perform physical activity. It also means having the energy and strength to feel as good as possible. Getting more fit, even a little bit, can improve your health." They go on to explain, "You don't have to be an athlete to be fit. Athletes reach a very high level of fitness. And people who take brisk half-hour walks every day reach a good level of fitness. Even people who can't do that much can work toward some level of fitness that helps them feel better and have more energy."

Group Health also advises their members, "When you stay active and fit you burn more calories, even when you are at rest. Being fit lets you do more physical activity, and it lets you exercise harder without as much work. It can also help you manage your weight. Improving your fitness is good for your heart, lungs, bones, muscles and joints. It lowers your risk for falls, heart attack, diabetes, high blood pressure and some cancers. If you already have one or more of these problems, getting more fit may help you control other health problems and make you feel better. Being more fit also can help you to sleep better, handle stress better and keep your mind sharp."

With exercise and fitness sounding like we finally found the "Fountain of Youth," how much do we need to achieve health-related fitness? Professionals in the health and fitness industry recommend goals including one or a combination of the following:

- ☆ **Do some sort of moderate aerobic activity, like brisk walking, for at least 2 1/2 hours per week.**
  - You may spread these 150 minutes any way you like, i.e., 30 minute walks 3 days per week and 15 minute walks the other 4 days per week. Or, take a 45 minute walk every other day.

- ☆ **Do more vigorous activities, like running, for at least 1 1/4 hours per week.**
  - Run for 25 minutes 3 times per week, or, run for 15 minutes 5 times each week.

How do you know if your exercise program is within the proper band of effort to achieve your fitness goals? First, check with your doctor to determine a safe, yet productive exercise plan. A good starting point is to know your maximum target heart rate. This is normally calculated by deducting your age from the number 220. For example, if you are age 70, deduct that from 220, giving you a maximum heart rate of 150. Your beginning target might be to do exercises elevating your pulse or heart rate to only 50% to 60% of your maximum target heart rate. You may then, over time, increase your heart rate to 70% to 80% of your maximum target rate. For the above example, this could mean initially keeping your heart rate between 75 and 90 beats per minute, gradually working up to a pulse rate of 105 to 120. The critical importance is to **keep your doctor advised** about your exercise program, particularly if you have not exercised for a long time.

The three main types of fitness are:

- ☆ Aerobic or Cardio (Endurance) which gauges how well your body utilizes oxygen. This depends on the condition of your heart, lungs and muscles. Any exercise which makes your heart beat faster, such as walking, cycling or running, can improve aerobic fitness.
- ☆ Muscle fitness (Strength) means building stronger muscles and increasing how long you can use them. Activities like weight lifting, resistance training and push-ups improve your muscular fitness.
- ☆ Flexibility is what allows your joints and muscles to move through their full range of motion. Stretching before and after aerobic and strength training helps your body maintain its flexibility.

You don't need an expensive gym membership or personal coach to improve your physical activity.

Incorporate physical activity in your daily life:

- ☆ Use the stairs.
- ☆ Walk to errands.
- ☆ Park away from the store when you shop.

Start a walking program:
- ☆ Buy a pedometer to count your steps.
- ☆ Walk 30 minutes of your lunch hour, if you work.
- ☆ Join a walking group or walk with a partner.

Schedule your activity:
- ☆ Break your routine into three 10-minute walks if you lack the time for one 30-minute walk.
- ☆ Use the mall if you wish to avoid walking in the rain.

Find an activity you enjoy:
- ☆ Vary the activity so you don't get bored.
- ☆ Sports like tennis and racket ball keep you interested.
- ☆ A rowing machine or compact treadmill, allowing you watch TV as you exercise, can eliminate boredom.

Set small, realistic goals:
- ☆ Record results with speed or distance meters.
- ☆ Reward yourself each time you achieve a goal.

For anyone with a little competitive inclination, make fitness fun through something like the *Senior Games.* Every state has annual competitive events for ages 55 and up. I cover this more fully in **Chapter Eleven—Affordable Fun,** describing ways to put fun into your fitness program.

The laws of physics still apply to exercise and fitness for, **"A body in motion tends to stay in motion, while a body at rest tends to stay at rest."** Like any other new routine, it takes a least 21 days of your preferred activity to lock it in as a habit. This can work both ways, for if you quit exercising for 21 days, you tend to use this as your new habit. Make every effort to develop a program you will follow, without fail, for at least 21 days, to get your good habits established.

Bill Gavin, M.D., has developed a workable program, as documented in his book, *No White At Night,* to help you adjust your lifestyle and improve your health. Dr. Gavin's basic degree is in Internal Medicine, with his specialty in Cardiovascular Medicine. He heads the Providence Medical Group-Cardiology Division of Olympia, Washington's Providence St. Peter Hospital. Dr. Gavin's own body weight challenges, plus a diabetic mother, facing weight and health risks, caused him to document a successful weight control and lifestyle program. His program is utilized by Dr. Gavin, his mom, his patients and the readers of his book. The book is still available at Amazon.com. He has successfully combined the elements of exercise, fitness and diet to achieve the ideal approach to your health.

Dr. Gavin, like many of us, had no problem with weight control until he was around 35 years old. He then seemed to gain about 3 to 5 pounds per year, until reaching an unacceptable weight. He increased his exercise, but that didn't work. He continued what he described as a "low fat" American Heart Association diet, but it was not really a low calorie diet. He relates two memories of this diet; he didn't lose much weight and he was always hungry. Something different had to happen, so he kept up his exercise program, and then began following some of the principles of *The Zone Diet*. He had good success over the first year, losing 35 pounds, although he did not weigh his food and perform the many calculations the *Zone Diet* called for.

Nearly 30 percent of Dr. Gavin's patients required counseling in weight loss and diet, but most found the group meetings, *Weight Watchers* specialty foods and unfamiliar recipes difficult to consistently follow. Most drifted back to their old habits, gaining back all or a portion of the weight lost. Dr. Gavin decided a change to a sustainable lifestyle for himself and his patients was needed. Something that was simple, yet effective. He pulled together his knowledge of other diet and exercise plans, his own experience, his mother's diabetic challenges, plus the results of his patient's attempts at weight control. The outcome is the *No White At Night* lifestyle program.

Dr. Gavin utilized a version of the *Zone Diet*, with about 40 percent carbohydrate, 30 percent protein and 30 percent fat, as the most effective diet. He then developed his weight control lifestyle from there. The popular diets vary all over the ball park in their approach. From the low carbohydrate-high fat Atkin's diet, recommending 5 percent carbohydrate, 35 percent protein and 59 percent fat, to the American Heart Association diet, with 55 percent carbohydrate, 18 percent protein and 30 percent fat. Dr. Gavin determined the *Atkin's Diet* could lead to excessive cholesterol for many, plus it was difficult to maintain over longer periods of time. The high carbohydrate *American Heart Association* diet caused many followers to gain weight due to the higher caloric intake.

Dr. Gavin's program evolved into, **The Three Rule Diet**. He advises, "You won't have to weigh or measure food on a regular basis with this diet, but you will need to be aware of what you are eating, so read the labels."

Rule 1. Eat Three Meals a Day:

Skipping meals at breakfast or lunch sets you up for weight gain, as studies on animals have found. An exemplary study used two sets of lab rats, which were fed the same number of calories each day. One group had the calories spread over three equal meals per day, while the second group had the same calories in one meal at the end of the day. The three meal group maintained normal body weight, while the one meal group became fat. We're not rodents, but the same principle applies. Skipping earlier meals creates hunger and heavier eating later in the day, with little time to burn off the calories before bedtime.

He ranks the importance of meals as: breakfast, first, lunch, second and dinner, last. The unfortunate thing is, if we skip only one meal, it tends to be breakfast. The common excuse is, "I just don't have time." Dr. Gavin's response is, "Try eating peanut butter on a piece of toast."

This requires very little time, and it provides a relatively good balance between carbohydrate, protein and fat. His belief is, "By eating breakfast you fire up your metabolic engine and make it easier for your body to burn excess fat."

Rule 2. Eat Some Lean Protein with Every Meal:

The challenge is to find a suitable protein you like, whether it is meat, fish, fowl or a vegetable source like peanut butter or soy butter. Dr. Gavin has identified a number of lean proteins, such as, egg whites, peanut butter, smoked fish, Canadian bacon, lean lunchmeat, nonfat yogurt, low-fat cottage cheese and mozzarella cheese, plus many other types of meat, fish and fowl. If you have concerns regarding chemically processed meats, concentrate more on the natural fish, fowl and meat.

He stresses eating protein to keep from getting hungry between your normal meals. Proteins are one of the most effective foods in curbing hunger. Fat is the second best food type to slow your digestion and control hunger. Carbohydrates are the least effective food in controlling hunger, allowing hunger pangs to hit long before your next meal is scheduled. Hunger pangs, causing snacking between meals, is the bane of the dieter. Avoid falling into this trap by adopting the *Three Rule Diet*. Dr. Gavin's book has a number of excellent recipes which match the philosophies of his lifestyle program.

Rule 3. No White at Night:

In response to the question of, "What is the no white at night I'm to avoid?" Dr. Gavin explains this means, no rice, bread, potatoes or pasta, nor their variants. This includes no red potatoes, brown rice, whole-wheat bread and starchy vegetables such as corn, either white or yellow. He advises, "Dinner should become lean meat, fish or fowl and all of the salad and vegetables you want." He also suggests you not use table sugar and avoid milk at dinner as well.

Chapter Ten

Dr. Gavin emphasizes an important concept, "You can get fat eating nonfat foods." The question often arises, "Starch is a low fat food, why do we have to limit its intake?" His answer includes the example of how feed lots fatten cattle before they are sent to market. The cattle are kept in an inactive environment and fed low-fat grain. He explains the same principle works for us, as our wonderful bodies first turn our food to sugar for immediate use. When our level of activity does not require all of the sugar or glycogen available, rather than waste the energy, it converts the sugar to fat for future energy needs.

To build your muscles you must exercise and consume protein at the same time. People ask, "If carbohydrates and starches, along with fat, are causing my weight gain, how about just loading up on proteins? Also, isn't protein what I need to build up my muscles?" Dr. Gavin advises, "Do not assume that eating protein will build your muscles." You must have protein and exercise together to get the job done. Another important point he makes is the need to drink large amounts of water to lose weight. The human body needs a normal minimum of at least 1 liter of water per day, with most nutritional plans recommending 8 large glasses of water per day. When attempting to burn body fat, which weighs approximately a kilogram or 2.2 lbs. per 9000 calories, you need more water. Your body requires roughly 20 pounds of water to unlock the 2.2 pounds of fat.

Dr. Gavin quotes an old diet counselor's saying that summarizes his approach to successful dieting, "Eat breakfast like a king, lunch like a storekeeper and dinner like a pauper." In addition to the guidelines for your pattern of eating, an understanding of the concepts of Glycemic Index and Glycemic Load will help you succeed with your weight loss or maintenance. You'll find more information regarding the Glycemic Index and Load in diabetic literature.

The Glycemic Index is a measure of how fast your blood sugar rises after you eat a particular food. The faster your blood sugar rises;

the higher the Glycemic Index. Foods with high Glycemic Indexes produce a very high insulin response within your body. That insulin rise ultimately leads to hypoglycemia and hunger. Dr. Gavin's approach is, "Changing the high Glycemic Index carbohydrates in your diet at night from starches to vegetables or salad reduces your insulin level and helps promote weight loss."

The other important Glycemic factor is Glycemic Load. Glycemic Load is the measurement of the total carbohydrate or sugar in a given food group. An example of the variations would be comparing potatoes to carrots. Both have high Glycemic Indexes, but potatoes also have a high Glycemic Load. The higher the Glycemic Load the longer your blood sugar stays elevated. While carrots have a Glycemic Index nearly as high as potatoes, the low Glycemic Load allows your blood sugar to quickly return to normal after eating carrots. Carrots will not make you fat.

To learn more about Glycemic Index and Load, go to the Internet and search for Glycemic Index, and a number of helpful sites will appear. According to Dr. Gavin, a particularly good site is www.glycemicindex.com, which is maintained by the University of Sydney in Australia. Anyone with diabetes or diabetes tendencies should take the time to learn more about Glycemic Index and Load.

Dr. Gavin learned early in his weight loss endeavors, diet alone, or exercise alone, are not effective methods to lose and keep off serious weight reductions. To lose 30 pounds in a year requires burning 390 calories per day or reducing you calorie intake by this amount. He learned that the most workable plan was to drop caloric intake and increase exercise to total 390 calories per day. This will normally lead to a weight loss of 2 to 3 pounds per month. Be sure to develop a sustainable pattern of diet and exercise. If you hate your necessary lifestyle, you will not stay on program long enough to achieve your goals. Make it a challenge, but be reasonable.

Chapter Ten

Here are some caloric burn estimates:

Calories Expended for Various Activities*	
Standing	104 cal./hr.
Walking - 2 mph	264 cal./hr.
Walking - 3 mph	352 cal./hr.
Walking - 4.5 mph	484 cal./hr.
Jogging - 5.5 mph	814 cal./hr.
Biking - 6 mph	264 cal./hr.
Biking - 12 mph	451 cal./hr.
Swimming - 25 yds/min	302 cal./hr.
Jumping Rope	550 cal./hr.
Stair-climbing machine	300-600 cal./hr.
Elliptical trainer	300-600 cal./hr.
*Results for a 165 pound individual	

Combine some form of exercise caloric burn with a reduction of diet calories to total 390 calories per day.

Dr. Gavin has a prescription he provides for each patient attempting to improve their health and control the weight in their lives. His program combines the necessary elements of exercise and diet to improve the quality of our lives. The simple prescription reads:

LIFE EXTENSION PRESCRIPTION
  ☆ **Exercise - Walk one half hour per day**
  ☆ **Eat three meals per day**
  ☆ **Eat some lean protein with each meal**
  ☆ **No white at night**

Follow Dr. Gavin's principles to help keep your retirement long and healthy.

Chapter Eleven

Affordable Fun in Retirement

Sadly, within six months to a year after retirement, many retirees are uninspired and/or bored with life. Some just go back to work, while fortunately others find new pursuits to reactivate their lives. Enjoyable retirement, like most other important phases of our lives, requires planning to succeed. Remember, retirement is the beginning of the next 30 years of your life. Look back over the last 30 years and recall many of the activities and lifestyle changes you faced. You can anticipate just as many changes as you go forward, as you experienced during the previous 30 years, maybe more.

Expanded **travel in retirement is a goal** of many retirees, so I have devoted the entire next chapter to this subject. In this chapter, we'll explore numerous enjoyable activities which don't involve a lot of travel.

Now that you have cut the strings with your work-a-day world, it's the ideal time to research your "Bucket List" of affordable fun in retirement. If your life becomes boring, it's because you haven't tried. Your new freedom gives you the opportunity to accomplish things such as cutting 6 to 8 strokes from your golf handicap. The country club membership may be a little hard on your budget, but other options are available. Many excellent public courses have very favorable rates for seniors, starting as young as 55 years of age. The men's and women's clubs have annual dues under $100, with 18 hole weekday rates of less than $25, including cart. A full range of tournaments and activities are provided, with costs low enough for both partners of a family to afford to play, plus no food and beverage minimums are required. Our local club has range balls for one-half price for the senior members, so no excuse for not working to improve your game.

A handcraft hobby, such as quilting, may be high on your "Bucket List." Your grandkids will cherish grandma's special quilt, with a unique design for each of them. These will become the heirlooms for future generations. Perhaps you're hesitant, because you have not sewn items since high school home economics, but don't let this stop you. Every quilting store has classes for all levels of ability, plus weekend TV has many free quilting shows. Even if you just begin with a 2 foot by 3 foot wall hanging kit, the end results will be highly rewarding.

The woodworker of the family can now setup a woodshop in the basement or in the corner of the garage, and then make the sawdust fly. Wood turning on a lathe takes very little room, but the bowls, candlesticks, ball point pens, spinning wheel lamps, etc. are beautiful as gifts or keepsakes. A number of wood artists have found a ready market for their creations in trade shows or specialty retail outlets. A one-of-a-kind piece of furniture for your own home or the homes of your kids and grandkids can become conversation pieces for years to come. Any of your granddaughters will be thrilled to have their own cedar hope chest, made by grandpa.

Our retirement community has a coed group, varying from 12 to 20 seniors, learning to play the ukulele. What fun it is to watch players aged from 75 to 85, discussing how to get their arthritic fingers to reach for a B flat chord. Learning new chords, recalling songs from the 20's and 30's and generally, having a great time and a big laugh, is wonderful therapy. Many heated discussions occur over the merits of vintage koa instruments versus spruce top or solid mahogany. The retirees have developed an entire new outlook and vocabulary relating to their newfound hobby. The brain stimulation, learning a new instrument and the accompanying music, is an exceptional way to keep dementia at bay.

You are never too old to try something new. Our community also has a group of ladies learning belly dancing, with the oldest about 85. They have weekly lessons taught by a professional instructor, learning a number of routines. They perform at many of the other retirement communities in our area, having as much fun as do the spectators. They are also a popular act in the annual talent show. Theirs is the perfect activity, combining a learning process with excellent full body exercise. At the end of the one hour lesson, they are all perspiring and feeling they have had a true workout. Their practicing at home continues to provide a healthful and consistent exercise regimen.

What better time, than when retired, to write your memoirs. Don't be saddened, like many of us, when our parents are gone and we haven't a written record of their family history. Lack of writing experience should never hold you back, for today's communities have many resources to get you started documenting your history.

An excellent place to begin is on line at www.SoYouWantToWrite.com where you will meet Ann McIndoo, a world renowned author's coach. She has many affordable authorship materials and techniques, both on her website or at www.amazon.com. She has developed methods which do not even require a computer to achieve your memoir publication. Ms. Mcindoo helps you document your information, using a compact voice activated digital recorder. Your recordings are then given to manuscript typists for transcription into draft form and then into print. You can then correct and update the draft, and you will be ready, with Ann's guidance, to become a published author.

Most of our local community colleges and senior centers also have writing and publishing courses. Check their curriculum or go online to look for these resources. Your efforts will create a written record for your own kids and family to build upon. Once you provide the leadership, you'll be surprised how the rest of the family will expand and add to your material. Being the starter seems to break up the log jam, and more family history begins to flow. Family memoirs are an ideal way to provide a true legacy at a minimal cost.

Interesting stories by persons with unique summer employment, such as Park Rangers, Forest Service Fire Fighters or Alaska Fisherman, can bring wonderful stories to their readers. Young women, with summer work in remote Alaska fishing lodges, or at somewhere, such as Yellowstone National Park, are just a few potential ideas. Wild bear stories, plus naive tourists, can provide a wealth of interesting material. You might be surprised how others can live vicariously, through your adventures and experiences.

Gardening is another outstanding way to combine recreation, exercise and food in a single rewarding activity. Mel Bartholomew's books on *Gardening By the Square Foot*, are a fine resource to get you into the dirt. His approach can get you started, even without the space for the large garden patch used by our ancestors. A space as small as 4 feet by 4 feet is all that is needed, with 6 inch sidewalls filled with a rich, weed free soil mix. Divide the area into 12 inch squares and you are ready to garden. Mr. Bartholomew has many suggested seed patterns, but you can substitute your own best-liked crop plantings. It's wonderful to see how much fresh and wholesome produce can come from such a small area. If you have more space, expand your garden, including replacing flowers with vegetables. Many residents of apartments or condos, have access to community gardens or pea patches. If you raise more than you can use, donate to the local food bank.

Ballroom dancing, particularly with the popularity of *Dancing With The Stars*, is a fast growing activity among all ages. The multiple benefits of physical fitness and social interaction make this of special interest to seniors. Not only does it bring back fond memories of your younger years, but the additional benefits of exercise, while displaying more skills than your grandkids, is fun. The beauty of ballroom dancing is you don't need special equipment, other than a pair of comfortable and slippery shoes, plus the costs are minimal. Most senior centers have weekly or monthly dances, along with various ethnic groups, such as the Swedish Vasa or the Norwegian cultural centers. Typical costs are only $5 to $10 for an evening or afternoon of entertainment and exercise.

Fly fishing and fly tying are becoming special areas of interest for more and more persons. Whether in Alaska, Yellowstone National Park or close to your home, fly fishing gets you out in the fresh air. It provides you with solid exercise, while challenging you to outwit the wily trout, steelhead or salmon. It's a sport which is readily shared by men or women, so it provides great family fun. Nothing beats catching a fish on a fly you have tied yourself. Women are particularly adept at fly tying, with their handcraft experience and hand dexterity.

Downsizing your home to a condo or large RV will not limit your fly tying accomplishments, for all of your tools, supplies and a vise, can function on the corner of your dining room table. Portable fly tying kits can easily accompany you to a remote cabin, tent or lodge, allowing you to match patterns to the hatch on your favorite lake or stream. Tying a dozen special flies for your guide will definitely cause you to be fondly remembered the next time you wish to book an outing.

Lifetime hunters can use the knowledge and skills, gained over many years, for a new, bloodless sport of camera hunting. Instead of mounted trophies on your den wall, beautiful photos of wild game, photographed in their natural setting, can be priceless. In the past you would need a backpack full of cameras and lenses to film wildlife, but now, even some pocket sized cameras have 14 power lenses, with 14 megapixil quality. *National Geographic* style of photography still requires multiple gear costing $1,000's, but an amateur can achieve wonderful results on a limited budget. It can be much less costly than a hunting rifle and a high quality scope, plus the results can be much more rewarding.

The Senior Games have brought a whole new dimension to exercise and competition, for anyone over the age of 50. Each state has regional contests during the even numbered years, such as 2012, 2014 and 2016. The top 4 competitors in each event or anyone meeting minimum performance standards in the applicable events, qualify for the nationals. They are held in the odd numbered years, such as 2013, 2015 and 2017. Nationals are alternated between the various time zones, to equalize the necessary travels for the qualifiers. For many, this type of competition gives the incentive to stay in shape and maintain proper weight. Working out year around helps you meet the fitness goals covered in Chapter 10, plus you are ahead of most of your competition for the next games.

At Nationals, competition occurs in Archery, Badminton, Bowling, Cycling, Golf, Horseshoes, Pickleball, Race Walk, Racquetball, Road Race, Shuffleboard, Softball, Swimming, Table Tennis, Tennis, Track and Field, Triathlon and Volley Ball. To keep competition fair, all events are divided into 5 year age groups, i.e., 50-54, 55-59, 60-64, 65-69, etc., with the final grouping at 100+. One wonderful lady competed in the Track and Field Shot Put at age 104. She knew she would win a medal, because she would probably be the only one competing. She won!

Most all of the States have the National qualification events, but many have additional competition, such as Ping Pong, Billiards, Sailing, Rowing and others., The main thing is to remain competitive and stay in shape. To check for National Senior Games go on line to www.nsga.com where you will find schedules, results of priors games, plus a wealth of other information relating to the Senior Games. Websites are also available for each of the various State Senior Games held in the even years. Also, the logistics of putting on the games requires many helpers. Helping conduct the games can be a wonderful contribution to your community.

Restoration of environmentally sensitive areas is a national program. The success of this program requires a huge amount of volunteer labor. The Nisqually National Wildlife Refuge, at the mouth of Washington State's Nisqually River, is a current award winner in the Pacific Northwest. About 1.5 square miles of the Nisqually River Delta have been restored by removal of 1000's of feet of 100 year old pasture land dikes, activating miles of interconnected sloughs and back eddies, both saltwater and fresh water, with the development of trails and elevated board walks to access the Refuge. A large parking area and Visitor's Center have been added , along with wheel chair accessible paths, to accommodate the 1000's of visitors. Hundreds of additional acres are planned for restoration in the near future.

National, State and Local funds were used to acquire private lands within the refuge, but the most progress has been through volunteer efforts from members of the Nisqually Society. They work as docents, both in the Visitor's Center and as trail guides, as well as planters of native vegetation and restoration helpers. This is one of those projects where you feel good physically from the hard labor, in addition to how you feel emotionally from knowing you have contributed to a lasting and worthwhile program. Throughout North America many similar projects need the help of active and dedicated volunteers. Be involved. Be productive.

If you are fortunate to live near a college or university, their departments of anthropology are typically collecting artifacts and relics from Native American Societies that once resided in their region. Enrolling in an anthropology class or merely volunteering to help with a "dig" may involve you in a whole new hobby. Again, you can be rewarded with a combination of new knowledge and physical exercise.

You're never too old to entertain. What a way to stay young. Retirees who always wished to be on the stage, with skills of acting, dancing, singing or playing an instrument, have many opportunities in Community Theater. Once again, living in a community with a college or university, may provide a greater variety of theater programs. Around the area of Olympia, WA, with a population of 150,000, you have two large community theater groups, plus the community college, a state college and a small University, all supply performers to different theatrical productions. Almost all of the productions need some more mature actors and participants, both on stage and back stage.

The Olympia area also has an active group known as *Wrinkles of Washington*, or WOW, requiring performers to be at least age 55, but no upper age limit. They produce two musical comedies or musical shows each year. Most of the proceeds, over $20,000, go to support the local senior centers. Around 75 seniors have a blast performing in and producing these shows. A second group of local senior performers produce at least one show each year, known as the *Entertainment Explosion*. In Palm Springs, California, you'll find 60 to 85 year old, semi-retired professional dancers, singers and comedians, performing daily.

This chapter has just scratched the surface of the many healthful and enjoyable ways to have fun in your life after retirement. The main thing is to not get caught in a rut of sameness or inactivity, or to become bored with life. Retirement has the potential to be your most rewarding and productive phase of your life. You now have the flexibility of doing what you want to do, rather than what you have to do to earn a living. The most important thing is to do something, and to remain an active member of your community.

Strive to be the retiree participating in community events, pursuing new hobbies, being active in service clubs and volunteering to help youngsters, seniors without families or those in need. You will experience a wonderful, fulfilling life in retirement, and you will likely live at least the four score and ten, that was so unusual just 50 or 60 years ago.

Chapter Twelve

Travel in Retirement

High on most all retiree's "Bucket List" is the desire to travel. Whether Europe, Antarctica, Pacific Islands, Africa, South America, Alaska or North America, travel comes to the forefront of your goals. For many, cost is the main limiting factor for your travels. One way to maintain control of your nest egg budget, rank order your most desired travel destinations, and then make rough estimates of the various costs involved for each. Compute costs per day, plus transportation, and then add 20% to your estimate for a realistic total cost. These numbers will allow you to compare your various options, and how best to fit these travel goals into your retirement budget and cash flow. If you need to stretch your budget, consider close to home travels, interspersed with more expensive overseas excursions every three or four years,

Cruising is a wonderful way to see the world as long as you have a flexible timetable and several alternate locations to visit. It can be one of your most cost effective forms of travel, with the majority of your basic costs included in your total package. Deluxe accommodations, gourmet foods, intercity transportation and free onboard entertainment are all included. One caution, shore excursions, internet access, onboard drinks, both alcohol and non-alcohol and spontaneous shopping, can blow your budget. Set limits on purchases, buy small amounts of wine or other beverages on shore, plus only join shore excursions which are really of interest. Most stops allow exploring cities on foot, or use of local bus, rail or taxi transportation. Study excursions to look for the best values. Another great value is the free, onboard professional entertainment, which equals any of the Las Vegas lounge shows. The ship's casinos are another matter, for they have a high profit bias toward the house. Rick Steves, author of *Europe Through the Back Door*, feels, "Other than sleeping on a park bench, there is no more affordable way to see Europe than cruising."

If you are like most retirees, Alaska has a high priority on your "someday list." Seattle and Vancouver, B.C., are the main ports serving the Alaska trips, making your exploration of these two exciting cities, before or after your cruise, an excellent option. Both cities have hosted World Fairs, with residual developments adding to their sophistication and uniqueness. The Vancouver and Seattle airports have flights all over the world, so connections should not be a problem. When considering cruising that requires you to fly in or out of major cruise destinations, check with the cruise line for your airfare. Many cruise lines will provide the lowest cost airfares, when packaged with a particular cruise.

If Alaska is your first choice destination, much of your fun will be in advance planning for your adventure. The internet can be your best friend in researching for your visit. Determine which cruise lines serve this market by just searching for Alaska Cruises. You may find Carnival, Celebrity, Crystal, Disney, Holland America, Norwegian, Princess and others serving this desirable market. When in doubt as to the best cruise line, pick a company with which you have cruised before, if possible. Most cruise lines offer many incentives to attract repeat customers, such as the Holland America's Mariner's Society. You may be offered special rates for certain cruises, discounts for onboard purchases and exclusive parties and gatherings for the Mariner's members. Study the itinerary and maps of the various cruise packages, for there can be considerable variation. Alaska cruises, like most other regions, occur within a definite time of the year. Booking an early April or late September Alaska cruise may save you $100's, if not $1,000's.

Some seven day cruises, to or from Vancouver, B.C., will cross the Gulf of Alaska to Seward, on the Kenai Peninsula, allowing passengers to continue overland by bus or train to Anchorage and Fairbanks. You then fly out of Fairbanks or Anchorage to Vancouver or Seattle. An option is to fly to Fairbanks, spend seven days on the land tour, catching a southbound cruise ship from Seward to Vancouver. One of the best values for an Alaska cruise is an inside cabin on the seven day package between Seward and Vancouver, available for as little as $349.

Most of the 7 day cruises originating in Seattle are up and back, beginning and ending in Seattle. They normally visit Ketchikan, Sitka, Juneau and Skagway, all in Southeastern Alaska, plus U.S. Laws require the ship to visit a foreign port before returning to the U.S. This law causes Holland's ships to spend a day in delightful Victoria, the capitol of British Columbia, Canada. The lowest cost cabin for this itinerary is around $499, but no air fare is required from or to Alaska. The Veranda cabins, which are desirable when cruising Southeastern Alaska, can vary from $850 to $1700 each, so watch your week of travel. Ships from Vancouver always travel the southern portion of the Inside Passage, located between Vancouver Island and the British Columbia mainland, while Seattle ships use the Pacific Ocean, on the west side of Vancouver Island.

Other major cruise line ports include, Boston, MA, Ft. Lauderdale, FL, Los Angeles, CA, New Orleans, LA, New York, NY and San Diego, CA. The ports tend to serve specific markets, but some overlap occurs, so check for the easiest port to reach from your home. Cruising is very seasonal, so rates can vary greatly, depending on the time of year. Generally, the best values are found with the transiting cruises. These occur when the cruise line companies move their ships all over the world, depending on the seasons. When it's winter in the U.S. ships will serve South America, Australia and New Zealand, returning to Northern Hemisphere markets around April.

You may find transiting cruises priced 50% to 60% below their peak season rates. Retirees can take advantage of these special seasonal values, traveling from the U.S. to the Mediterranean, or from Ft. Lauderdale, through the Panama Canal to Seattle, for the Alaska trade. For longer transiting cruises consider San Diego to Australia, Ft. Lauderdale to Chile or Seattle/Vancouver, B.C. to the Orient, by way of Alaska.

Combining cruising during the shoulder season with transiting ships, is one of the best kept secrets within the cruise line industry. Fortunately, many seniors have the flexibility to take advantage of these available bargains. In 2011 a 23 day cruise in April, from Ft. Lauderdale, Florida, visiting Mediterranean ports in Portugal, Spain, France, Tunisia, Sicily and Italy, sold veranda staterooms for only $100 per person per day. Internet is your friend while researching the various itineraries and costs, but when you find a cruise of interest, check with your travel agent. Many times they will equal online rates, while handling all of the details.

Cruise lines have started extending their seasons in regions throughout the world. Service during some times of the year may bring foul weather into a cruise, so be cautious. Ellen Creager, of the *Detroit Free Press*, has published some guidelines for the best times to cruise in regions around the world. Her observations are:

- ☆ **Alaska:** Season runs April to September. Best is July and August. May or September can have rainy weather.
- ☆ **Antarctica:** Season runs November to March. Best is mid-December to February. Worst is November or March.
- ☆ **Caribbean:** The season is year-round, but the best is December to April. Worst is August to October, hurricane season. Cruise lines have flexible itineraries allowing hurricane season travel to be workable.

- ☆ **Mediterranean:** Season runs April to October, but now cruise ships are sailing year-round. Best is June or September (August is the most crowded). Worst is December to February.
- ☆ **New England:** Season runs April to October. Best is July to October. Worst is April to May.
- ☆ **Northern Europe:** Season runs May to September. Best is June through August. Worst is very early May.
- ☆ **Transatlantic:** Season runs March to November, with most repositioning cruises in spring and fall. Best is June to August. Worst is March or November.

Another enjoyable and economical way to travel is by using Bed and Breakfast or private inns for your accommodations. Your choices range from single bedrooms in a private home, to apartments , condos, or entire homes, depending upon your budget and size of your traveling group. San Francisco based **AirBnB** is among the largest and most experienced. Others to access for accommodations include, **Istopover, Roomarama** and **9flats**, plus, **HomeAway.com** for vacation rentals and entire homes around the world. **AirBnB** has a protective feature whereby they hold your deposit or advance rent money until you have actually seen the place where you will be staying. Only when you are satisfied the rental is as advertised are the funds released to the owner of the facility. All of the above are available through the internet, and they will provide references to help you prejudge the quality of their services.

Check the internet for reviews by previous B and B customers. These can provide clues to the pro's and con's of a particular rental. A B and B or small inn will keep you closer to the average citizen of the area you are visiting. Many inn keepers and B and B owners, met during your travels, may become lasting friends. In fact, it can seem as if you are staying with a friend or relative. The inn keeper can provide a wealth of local knowledge, helping you see the special sites without breaking your budget. The costs are usually much lower than using the large hotel chains.

Chapter Twelve

Airfare to your vacation destination may vary from 15% to 30%, depending on time of purchase and day of travel. Travel firms such as, Expedia, Travelocity and Orbitz found Tuesday was the best day to book a flight. This is based upon the majority of the airlines offering their specials for that week on Monday night. You will also find the best savings if you can travel on Tuesday, Wednesday or Saturday. Advance ticket purchase can be a saver, for the lowest priced seats tend to sell early. Buying a month or two in advance will typically give you the best seat choice and lowest rates. Red eye flights departing later at night, when traveling West to East, can save a night's lodging and provide an extra day of exploring your destination. Crossing the International date line, losing a day, plus following the sun to the West reduces some of the red eye benefits.

Efficient packing has become a new necessity, with the airlines charging for any checked luggage. If you can travel with only a carry-on, life becomes much simpler and cheaper. Rick Steves, European travel journalist, spends two, three week European trips per year, packing everything in a convertible back pack/carry-on. Here are a few tricks Steves and other experienced travelers recommend. First check the carry-on size allowance your airline permits. This typically is 22 to 24 inches long, 14 to 16 inches wide and 9 to 10 inches deep. Bring only two basic clothing colors, which should be compatible with each other, and only one pair of shoes, in addition to ones worn during travel. A shoe color such, as burgundy, usually blends with most clothing colors.

If you do have to check bags, a few cautions apply. Never leave valuables or electronics in you checked bag. Even with a carry-on, if you are late to the gate and must check your carry-on, remove any valuables and electronics before sending your bag to the luggage compartment. A uniquely colored ribbon, attached near the handle of your luggage, will make it easier to retrieve from the baggage claim area. Also, with many look alike bags, it will keep someone else from inadvertently taking your luggage. When on the plane, place your carry-on in the overhead bin across the isle, rather than above your seat. This allows better observation of your bag. Always have a business card or other ID within your luggage.

Rick Steves is a proponent of traveling throughout Europe by rail. He finds this mode of travel, "Less stressful, better for the environment and just plain friendly--offering a relaxed way to connect with traveling Europeans." Steves has found, "As I reflect on the ease of European train travel, the trains go where you need them to go and are fast, frequent and generally affordable (especially in the south). You can easily have dinner in Paris, sleep on the train and have breakfast in Rome, Munich or Madrid." Depending on your chosen level of railroad accommodations, European rail travel may seem a little pricey. But, from Mr. Steves' experience, "If you've never experienced 21st-century rail travel (and you haven't, if your experience is limited to rail travel in the U.S.), you may find that it's about the best travel deal going."

The railpass can be an excellent value. According to Rick Steves, "The railpass covers a specific geographical area (regional, country or multiple countries); it has a fixed number of travel days; and it's either a consecutive-day pass or a flexipass (allowing you more flexibility to spread out your travel days)." Choosing the best pass depends on your itinerary. If your plans call for every day travel, covering as much ground as possible, the consecutive-day pass is the way to go. Most travelers prefer the flexipass, where you have a certain number of travel days to use within a longer period of time. An example is purchasing a two month pass with 10 travel days. You can spread these days throughout the 60 day period, or you can use all 10 days consecutively. Rail travel may be worth a try.

When your budget says, "Let's stay close to home," many options are still available. Carol Pucci, *Seattle Times*, travel writer, found a new, economical intercity bus in the Pacific Northwest. The new system, known as the BoltBus, provides low-cost, nonstop travel between

Seattle, WA and Portland, OR, or between Seattle and Vancouver, B.C., Canada. As Carol noted, "This is not your grandmother's Greyhound." The bus has free Wi-Fi, leather seats and component plug-in outlets for each passenger.

The BoltBus guarantees at least one $1 seat on each trip, but typically fares vary from $8 to $25, depending on demand, the day of the week and how far in advance you book. Amtrak serves the same route, but charges $39 to $68 each way, according to how fast their seats book and when you make reservation. The train has discounts for students, children and seniors, along with AAA and AARP.

Although no food service is available, each bus has a clean bathroom, equipped with a small sink and hand-gel dispenser. The 170 miles from Seattle to Portland took just 3 hours, averaging about 55 mph. With the normal train delays, Amtrak usually covers the same distance in about 3 1/2 hours. This style of travel is spreading across the United States, so check on line in your area for similar operations. It's not often you can travel nearly 200 miles for little more than the cost of 2 gallons of gas—an intriguing alternative when traveling city center to city center.

Great savings are available at deluxe resort locations by scheduling your travels during the shoulder or slow seasons. For instance, most Hawaiian hotels and condos offer lower prices during early February, early March, late May, early June and in the fall. It is to their benefit to keep their rooms filled, so the favorable rates are offered. Most all resort areas have slow seasons, with discount rates to attract customers. Lodging, transportation and activities for 30 to 50% lower than peak season are worth considering, even when you have to alter your time table to enjoy the reduced costs. Booking Hawaii visits for mid-week travel is another example of how to save on your travel budget. Round trip coach fares between Seattle and Honolulu can vary from as little as $400 to nearly $800 within a 30 day period. Check at Kayak.com and Alaskair.com to find the best dates to travel within the shoulder or slow seasons.

Take advantage of your flexible schedule to achieve savings and travel more for less. An excellent approach to achieve your best values is to first find the lower cost travel dates, and then locate accommodations to fit these dates. Also, before booking specific reservations, check with the most active airlines serving the market within which you wish to travel. You may find prices for a package, including airfare, accommodations and a car, for less than you can book the individual piece parts. Use the internet to help you save $100's.

Travels within North America can be a cost effective and enlightening experience. One of the best values to help you obtain these savings is the Golden Age Passport, which provides free access to nearly 2000 federally managed recreational facilities, included all of our National Parks. Up to 3 additional adults and any children age 16 and under, within your vehicle, are also admitted free. This $10 pass is available to any U.S. senior aged 62 and older.

You don't have to be a gambler to enjoy the resort cities of Las Vegas, Reno/Tahoe and Atlantic City. With the competition from Indian casinos across the U.S., these original gambling meccas have become more and more family oriented, end destination resorts. Subsidized by gambling revenues, the food, lodging and entertainment are some of the most reasonable in the Nation.

Once again, a retiree's flexibility in choosing a time to travel, may give you the best savings in our gambling communities. Pick a shoulder season, such as February, March, late September, October, late November and early December. Access a particular hotel/casino and you will usually find a rate calendar covering 3 or 4 months, during a period you wish to travel. Rates can vary by 35% to 50% depending upon the resort's expected seasonal demand, plus any scheduled major conventions or special events.

Treat gambling as a recreation, and don't believe you can consistently win against the house. A favorite saying I've heard is, "They didn't build

Chapter Twelve

those casino palaces from selling mixed nuts." If you play long enough the house will beat you, for the gambling odds are in their favor. **You may win in the short run, but eventually the house will get you.** With this fact in mind, be a good money manager, and don't lose more than you can afford.

The ideal approach is to maintain the gambling as a small part of your visit, and instead, enjoy the special ambiance of the casino community. Atlantic City, located on the New Jersey shore has a unique feeling of its own. Walk the Board Walk, visit the shops and peddlers for souvenirs, take advantage of the happy hours and food specials, and bring home many lasting memories. Atlantic City is in the center of some of the most populated areas of the United States, so carefully pick your time to visit.

Las Vegas, a small desert town on steroids, has become, along with Macao in China, the largest gambling center in the world. Downtown Las Vegas still retains many followers, with its nightly Laser Light Show, reasonably priced accommodations and casinos located within an easy walk of each other. South of town is the casino growth area of glitzy, high rise casinos, known as the Las Vegas Strip. The billions of dollars spent on the huge casinos has caused the "house" to retain a little more of the gambler's money. Less liberal odds on their slot machines and higher minimum bets and tighter odds on the table games, keep gambling a little more expensive than in Reno, Nevada.

The large casino shows are beautiful but expensive. The excellent lounge entertainment, available throughout Las Vegas, are great budget stretchers. You may see 3 or 4 lounge shows for the price of one of the extravagances. Free, family styled entertainment abounds in Las Vegas, with sidewalk viewing of volcanoes and pirate ship battles, plus free circus acts at the Circus Circus Casino. Food prices vary from reasonable to very expensive, with buffet dining available everywhere. Buffets can stretch you budget, but they can also stretch your waist line. One trick is to eat a heavy, breakfast buffet and then a late lunch, with a happy hour, and skip dinner. You will have consumed all of your recommended calories, plus you have stayed within your budget.

Of the three major casino communities within the U.S., Reno/Tahoe, Nevada, is probably the most family friendly location. The area is located in northwestern Nevada, close to the California border. Natural beauty and recreation abounds throughout the region.

Lake Tahoe, about 50 miles from Reno, is one of the most picturesque settings of Northern California and Northern Nevada. The 22 mile long, 12 mile lake forms a portion of the California-Nevada border. At approximately 6000 foot elevation, the lake is the source of the Truckee River. The river flows 120 miles from Lake Tahoe, through Reno and Sparks, to end as the main water supply to Pyramid Lake. Casinos are located in the northeast and southeast corners of the lake, all in Nevada. The California side of the lake has most of the private vacation homes and rental properties. Outdoor recreation of water, golf and snow sports, along with indoor recreation of gambling, keep the Lake Tahoe active year around.

The Reno/Sparks communities are the main hub of Northern Nevada gambling. Fifteen to 25 story casinos are found throughout the area, but not to the density and opulence of Las Vegas. Reno calls itself, "The Biggest Little City in the World." Gambling is a little more customer friendly, with better slot machine payouts and less expensive table games. Room rates, food and entertainment are considerably less costly than Las Vegas or Atlantic City.

Northern Nevada, around Reno/Sparks and Lake Tahoe, has a long history of gold and silver mining. A wonderful family day trip from Reno to the historic mining town of Virginia City, takes you over the 6800 foot Geiger Summit. The roads are all paved, but the narrow, windy route is a slow drive, which will take at least 45 minutes to travel the 23 miles from

Reno. Allow an hour or two to explore the town, with interesting shops and exhibits. A drink in the Bucket of Blood saloon is a must. Some of the richest silver mines in the United States were in this area.

Continue on toward Carson City, the State Capitol of Nevada. You will pass through remnants of old mining claims and small mining villages. Many signs of current mining activity are apparent, with the price of gold creating renewed interest in "Striking it rich." Carson City has an outstanding mining museum, with a recreated mine you may walk through. The mine shaft provides a safe, yet authentic feel of what it was like to work underground. The entire loop from Reno to Virginia City, on to Carson City, returning to Reno is only about 66 miles, but in historic terms it covers more than a century.

A well thought out travel agenda, with research and setting of priorities, can be one of your most rewarding segments of retirement living. A compact camera, photo travel albums and a simple journal will help you retain many fond memories of your journeys. These momentous will be lasting records of your happy travel times, as well as a legacy for your kids.

Chapter Thirteen

Plan Your Estate

As important as wills are to our personal estates, recent studies have found **over one-half of the U.S. population do not have wills**. The estates of our Hispanic population are even more at risk, with about three out of four individuals lacking wills. Without a will the laws of the state, within which you reside, will determine how your estate is distributed, without regard to your wishes. Don't let the courts and the political lawmakers determine how your estate will be settled.

Even though our demise is the destiny of each of us, a loved one's death is one of the most traumatic events in any family. With this in mind, the best legacy you can provide is to make the settling of your estate go as smoothly as possible. We have all known of the hate and discontent some families have experienced when a deceased individual fails to plan ahead for his or her inevitable death. This chapter will provide ideas for how you can create an estate plan, authorizing the orderly distribution of assets and settling of your finances. Your goal should be to develop a fair and business-like estate plan. The most important thing to accept is, **"Our lives can end at any time."** For instance, none of the 45,000 persons killed in U.S. auto accidents each year were expecting their lives to end so soon. **EXACT A WILL NOW!**

Chapter Thirteen

Your estate plan is a very personal and individualistic program, and doesn't allow a "One size fits all" approach. Many estate do-it-yourself publications and web sites exist, and may help you gain substantial understanding, as you go through the exercise of your own planning. But, once you have put together tentative wills, etc., have a knowledgeable professional review all of your work. Your professional can check for state and federal estate law variations, look for ways to improve your efforts, and perhaps most importantly, advise you as to what legal documents you should execute, in addition to a will. Your documents must stand up in the legal world of probate and settlement of your estate. It is money well spent obtaining proper legal advice.

Attempting to save a few hundred dollars by developing your own estate plan may cost your estate and heirs many thousands of dollars. In reality, working with an estate planning specialist from the beginning will be your best investment. By the time you reach retirement age, you likely will have an attorney, as well as tax and financial advisors. Now is the time to draw on your relationships with these individuals. If your attorney is not experienced in estate planning, obtain his or her referral to an estate specialist. If your estate attorney and financial advisor are not up-to-date on the tax ramifications of estate planning, again, get referrals. You risk too much when relying only on "Do-it-yourself" estate planning.

Whether you plan to do the entire estate planning process yourself or work with specialists, review the 25 following suggestions. Utilize any which fit your circumstances. These are provided by the Dallas, Texas, legal firm of Web and Web, P.C.:

ESTATE PLANNING

1. **Make or update your will.** A will allows you to determine what happens to your money and possessions when you die, and who becomes the guardian of your minor children. Otherwise, state laws and courts make those decisions for you.

2. **Make a living will.** This document can speak for you by outlining the medical procedures you want taken if you become too ill to state your wishes yourself.
3. **Create durable powers of attorney.** These documents allow you to appoint someone to make decisions on your behalf if you become incapacitated. There are two types; one to deal with your personal, legal and financial affairs, and another to deal with health-care decisions.
4. **Create a letter of instructions.** This document provides a list of instructions for your survivors to follow. For example, it can spell out funeral wishes, people to contact, and where your will and other key papers can be found. It also can provide information about your financial accounts and activities. Be sure to include the necessary passwords and safe combinations to allow access to your information.
5. **Calculate your net worth, including life insurance proceeds.** If you have substantial net worth, consider talking to a tax or financial adviser to determine steps necessary to minimize or eliminate the impact of federal and state estate taxes.
6. **Establish a trust if appropriate.** A trust is a legal entity that holds property designated by you for the benefit of you and your beneficiaries. For example, you might need to set up a trust if you name minor children as your life insurance beneficiaries (legally they are too young to receive proceeds directly).
7. **Consider funeral preplanning.** Preplanning can relieve stress on your survivors and give you control over the ultimate cost of your funeral. If you are a U.S. military veteran, you may want military honors at your service, contact your local funeral home or military installation to check on eligibility and availability.
8. **Make arrangement for the orderly transfer of business assets.** Business owners can predetermine what will happen to assets through legal agreements and life insurance on business partners.

INSURANCE PLANNING

9. **Buy or update your life insurance.** Life insurance provides an immediate source of cash that can be exempt from federal and state income tax (but, in general, not estate taxes). It is important to review your ownership, beneficiary and coverage amount every two or three years to make sure your policies still reflect your needs and wishes.
10. **Consider buying health/medical insurance.** There are three major types of coverage that help protect and stretch your assets. Long-Term Care enables you to cover the cost of long-term care in your home or at a long-term care facility. Major Medical protects you against the ever-rising cost of medical care, and Disability helps protect your income if you no longer can work.
11. **Review your pension plan's survivor benefits.** This might be a plan offered through your employer or the military's Survivor Benefit Plan (SBP). SBP choices made at retirement can be changed if you divorce or marry. Also, the government periodically offers open enrollment periods that enable the plan owner to make changes.
12. **Review your IRA, 401(k) and other retirement plans** for beneficiary arrangements and benefits.

ORGANIZING FINANCIAL RECORDS

NOTE: If you store any of the following information on your computer, make a list of all passwords, plus indicate where any diskettes are stored and where the information can be found.

13. **Create a list of financial accounts.** List account numbers and pertinent information about your investments, bank accounts, insurance policies (life, disability, homeowners, credit and LTC) and other financial matters.
14. **List the location of valuable documents.** Your list might include deeds, car titles, military records, birth and marriage certificates, divorce decrees, passports and estate planning documents.

15. **List your personal data.** This can include your Social Security number, driver's license number, VA claim number, your date of birth and the names and phone numbers of family members.
16. **Arrange for access to your safe-deposit box or safe.** In many states, safe-deposit boxes are closed upon death and are not opened until probate. Make sure copies of your will and other important documents are available outside of your safe-deposit box.
17. **List loan documents and payments.** This listing should include information about credit cards, mortgages, and consumer loans, and auto and personal loans.
18. **List other income sources and government benefits.** This includes pensions and Social Security. For information on military benefits, check with the Veteran's Administration or you nearest military installation's casualty assistance office.
19. **List the location of tax records.**
20. **Verify account ownership and beneficiary designations.** Check financial accounts and insurance policies to make sure these conform to your estate planning arrangements.
21. **List all organizations in which you have membership.** They may provide special death benefits and should be noted for your survivors.

PERSONAL PLANNING

22. **Provide a trusted family member or friend** with the location of confidential or valuable items you may have put away for safekeeping.
23. **Provide a family member or friend** with the location of spare keys and security codes.
24. **Provide easy access to your will and your durable powers of attorney.** Keep signed, original copies in your attorney's office as well as a copy in a fireproof file at home. Also, give a signed copy to your executor.
25. **Provide the name of your veterinarian and care instructions for pets,** if appropriate.

Chapter Thirteen

The answers to the above questions and suggestions will assist your attorney as well as your estate administrator.

When putting together your estate plan, many times you are hiring an attorney by the hour. If you can streamline the process, helping your legal advisor's time be more productive, it will save you money. Other attorneys will help create your will and related estate planning documents on a flat fee basis. Most estate planning attorneys have check lists and "fill in the blanks" forms to help you provide the necessary data for your estate plan. Many times your attorney will provide data forms developed by your local State Bar Association. Their main goal is acquire the necessary information to develop the correct estate plan for each of you and your heirs.

Your estate attorney will incorporate the information from the 25 estate planning suggestions, plus additional documentation from your "fill-in-the blank" forms. You will need separate information for both husband and wife, for each will have their own separate estate plans. Your state laws and attorney's guidance will help you decide which documents are necessary. Generally, the following are considered:

☆ Community property agreement options:
- Specific properties may be identified.
- All community property, with no conversion.
- Conversion of separate properties to community.

☆ Durable Power of Attorney.
☆ Living Will.
☆ Prenuptial agreement, if applicable.
☆ Funeral preferences.

You, as principal, may sign an agreement, giving someone Power of Attorney to act in your behalf. Powers of Attorney can vary from taking effect immediately, in the future or at a future event, such as your death or incapacity. Power of Attorney agreements are so important, seek legal advice before creating them. The powers are as diverse as:

- ☆ Making health care decisions
- ☆ Buy or sell things
- ☆ Manage a business
- ☆ Invest money
- ☆ Cash checks
- ☆ Manage financial matters generally
- ☆ Sue on behalf of the principal

A very important decision when establishing any estate plan is the choice and appointment of a Fiduciary, such as an Administrator or Executor/Executrix, to direct the settlement of your estate. This person will be responsible for handling all of your estate's assets and obligations during the estate settlement process. The Powers of Attorney may cause your fiduciary to become involved while you are still living, depending upon the responsibilities identified in the Powers of Attorney. The Administrator has very demanding and time consuming duties, requiring sound judgment and trust of the heirs. Choose wisely.

If your estate has any value at all, create a will and the related documents. The results of your efforts may be the best legacy you can provide your family. If you live in a community property state, and there is a surviving spouse, most assets are allowed to pass directly to that person. In many community property states, a community property agreement, which can supersede the will, is necessary for the community property to pass to the spouse. This can greatly simplify settlement of your estate, but be certain your attorney agrees that you are not missing any critical steps. Even without assets, it is important your family knows your wishes regarding medical care, living will and funeral preferences.

Chapter Fourteen

Benefits of Giving Back

As you approach or enter the retirement phase of your life, you will recognize many of your lifetime achievements were accomplished through the support of others. The huge investment made in you by your parents is just one example. Teachers, relatives, friends, plus community infrastructure built by others, all played major roles in your life. Now is your time to pay back for all of their support, and to use your skills to help others.

Azim Jamal and Harvey McKinnon, in their book, *The Power of Giving*, make the point, "No matter what your circumstances in life, you have the ability to give." They continue by identifying how this is good for you and provides the following benefits:

☆ It can make a positive difference for others.
☆ There are emotional, physical and even financial benefits to you.
☆ It can help you achieve your full potential.
☆ It can bring you more meaning, fulfillment and happiness.

We seldom relate volunteering and philanthropy to good health, but as early as 1988 the May issue of *American Health* found the following benefits of giving and volunteering:

☆ Enhances your immune system,
☆ Lowers cholesterol levels,
☆ Strengthens your heart,
☆ Decreases the incidence of chest pains, and
☆ Generally reduces stress.

Jamal and McKinnon believe, "The world can be a different and better place if, while you are here, you give of yourself." They suggest you make a decision to have a positive impact on the lives of others, even if they are strangers. They found statistics indicating areas of needs throughout the world, such as:

☆ One out of every four people in the world is starving.
☆ As many as 1.5 billion people in the world do not have enough clean water.
☆ At least 20 million people are suffering the horrors of war, imprisonment and torture.
☆ Every few seconds a child dies from a preventable disease.
☆ One-seventh of the world's population is illiterate.
☆ In the United States, the world's richest country, 3 million people are homeless each year.

In addition to the needs in the foreign lands of the world, opportunities to serve in your own communities are everywhere. Service clubs such as Rotary, Kiwanis or Lions have hundreds of ongoing volunteer projects, providing you an easy way to serve. Rotary's support of the Boys and Girls Clubs, plus administering polio vaccine throughout the world, Kiwanis' children's camps or Lions' recycling of eye glasses are just a few samples. No special skills are needed in order to volunteer, or as Erwin Tan, M.D., director of Senior

Chapter Fourteen

Corps states, "If you have a passion, we have a purpose and a program for you."

"Boomers are the healthiest, best educated generation to transition through middle age to retirement," according to Dr. Tan, geriatrician. A recent change by the Senior Corps, to encourage more Boomers to be involved as senior companions, was to lower its age requirement from 60 to 55. The companions help older adults with shopping visits and medical appointments: as foster grandparents who mentor youth; and as volunteers at Coming of Age, which supports social service programs and conducts workshops on job and volunteer opportunities.

Coming of Age is also known as the Retired Senior Volunteer Program or RSVP in many states or communities. Their role is to be the conduit between the volunteers and the volunteering needs of the community. The waves of Boomers hitting age 65 after 2010, with their retained energy and resourcefulness, are the fastest growing segment of Coming of Age and RSVP. These new members, with their passion and enthusiasm, are taking "giving back" to new levels of success.

Your opportunities to help are unlimited. One local RSVP office is lining up volunteers for the following:

☆ Reading buddies for school districts.
☆ Host monthly wine and cheese tasting event.
☆ Office help in a learning-based organization.
☆ Help in Habitat For Humanity Retro Store.
☆ Read to children in child care centers.
☆ Receptionist for a senior center.
☆ Teach values of waste management at farmer's market.
☆ An adult education tutor.
☆ Guide at a new children's hands-on museum.
☆ Critical areas restoration project volunteer.

When volunteering you are fulfilling a need within your community, while personally reaping the benefits of giving back. Most non-profit, volunteer based organizations need financial help. But, as you can see from the preceding list of needs, most need your time as much as your money. Contact your local RSVP, Coming of Age or United Way office to learn of unlimited opportunities to serve. The important thing is to stay active in retirement, not only physically, but with your brain. Challenging volunteering is a win-win way of achieving this.

Chapter Fifteen

Workable Retirement Philosophies

Your spouse or partner is the most important person in your life. Don't allow a job, volunteering, your kids or your friends come ahead of your spouse or partner. If each of you give 110%, your life and retirement cannot help but succeed.

Maintain family ties. As your kids marry and relocate, work hard to keep lines of communication open. Social media, cell phones, Skype, email and snail mail allow easy contacts, but you still must make the effort. A calendar listing birthdays, anniversaries, etc., with appropriate cards sent, will mean a great deal to the recipients. As we age we don't need more things, but a card with a few thoughtful comments or notes of thanks can be the best gift ever.

Family gatherings maintain lasting ties and retains family history. Help your grandkids know their aunts, uncles, grandparents and cousins. Continue family reunions whenever possible.

You have a lifetime of experience, both good and bad. Use this knowledge to advise when asked, but don't push. Instead, encourage and mentor your kids and grandkids, whether in education, sports or jobs. Attend family sporting, graduation or recognition events as often as possible.

Maintain your health so you can enjoy life to the fullest. Keep your weight reasonable, eat healthy foods and don't wait until you are sick before you see your doctor.

Give back to your community, whether volunteering, service club membership, non-profit organizations or donations. The community has served you through the years, now it's your opportunity to pay back.

Document your family history as a legacy for your kids and grandkids.

Knowledge is treasure. Read, study and discuss. Your brain will rust from non-use, so keep it bright and shiny with expanded knowledge.

LIFE IS FUN. ENJOY IT!

Resources

Free websites to help with the financial side of retirement:

- ☆ www.ameriprise.com
- ☆ www.analyzenow.com
- ☆ www.fidelity.com
- ☆ www.msn.com/retirement
- ☆ www.vanguard.com/retirementplanning

Overseas living options:

- ☆ www.expatexchange.com provides a good overview of the challenges and benefits of living in other countries.

Continuing Care Retirement Communities:

- ☆ www.CARF.org for CARF International, which is a rating agency for CCRC's across the United States and Canada.
- ☆ www.panoramacity.org is one of the outstanding CCRC's in North America, and it is also my home for the last 13 years.

Check my resources page at www.jimrolson.com
for updates and new resources.